Copyright © 2011 XAMonline, Inc.
All rights reserved. No part of the material protected by this copyright notice may be reproduced or utilized in any form or by any means, electronic or mechanical, including photocopying, recording or by any information storage and retrievable system, without written permission from the copyright holder.

To obtain permission(s) to use the material from this work for any purpose including workshops or seminars, please submit a written request to:

XAMonline, Inc.
25 First Street, Suite 106
Cambridge, MA 02141
Toll Free: 1-800-509-4128
Email: info@xamonline.com
Web: www.xamonline.com
Fax: 1-617-583-5552

Library of Congress Cataloging-in-Publication Data

Wynne, Sharon A.
    TExES Generalist EC-6 191 Essentials Edition Practice Test 2: Teacher Certification /
    Sharon A. Wynne. -1st ed.
    ISBN: 978-1-60787-278-8
    1. TExES Generalist EC-6 191 Essentials Edition Practice Test 2   2. Study Guides
    3. TExES   4. Teachers' Certification & Licensure   5. Careers

Disclaimer:
The opinions expressed in this publication are the sole works of XAMonline and were created independently from the National Education Association, Educational Testing Service, or any State Department of Education, National Evaluation Systems or other testing affiliates.

Between the time of publication and printing, state specific standards as well as testing formats and website information may change that is not included in part or in whole within this product. Sample test questions are developed by XAMonline and reflect similar content as on real tests; however, they are not former tests. XAMonline assembles content that aligns with state standards but makes no claims nor guarantees teacher candidates a passing score. Numerical scores are determined by testing companies such as NES or ETS and then are compared with individual state standards. A passing score varies from state to state.

Printed in the United States of America   œ-1
TExES Generalist EC-6 191 Essentials Edition Practice Test 2
ISBN: 978-1-60787-278-8

Elementary Education
Post-Test Sample Questions

READING

1. **To make an inference a reader must:**
   (Average)

   A. Make a logical guess as to the next event

   B. Find a line of reasoning on which to rely

   C. Make a decision based on an observation

   D. Use prior knowledge and apply it to the current situation

2. **Which of the following is NOT utilized by a reader when trying to comprehend the meaning behind the literal text?**
   (Rigorous)

   A. Pictures and graphics in the text

   B. Background knowledge about a topic

   C. Knowledge of different types of text structure

   D. Context clues

3. **Phonological awareness includes all of the following skills except:**
   (Average)

   A. Rhyming and syllabification

   B. Blending sounds into words

   C. Understanding the meaning of the root word

   D. Removing initial sounds and substituting others

4. **Asking a child if what he or she has read makes sense to him or her, is prompting the child to use:**
   (Average)

   A. Phonics cues

   B. Syntactic cues

   C. Semantic cues

   D. Prior knowledge

5. Which of the following indicates that a student is a fluent reader?
   (Rigorous)

   A. Reads texts with expression or prosody

   B. Reads word-to-word and haltingly

   C. Must intentionally decode a majority of the words

   D. In a writing assignment, sentences are poorly-organized, structurally

6. If a student has a poor vocabulary the teacher should recommend that:
   (Rigorous)

   A. The student read newspapers, magazines, and books on a regular basis

   B. The student enroll in a Latin class

   C. The student writes the words repetitively after looking them up in the dictionary

   D. The student use a thesaurus to locate synonyms and incorporate them into his/her vocabulary

7. To decode is to:
   (Average)

   A. Construct meaning

   B. Sound out a printed sequence of letters

   C. Use a special code to decipher a message

   D. None of the above

8. John Bunyan, Coleridge, Shakespeare, Homer, and Chaucer all contributed to what genre of literature?
   (Average)

   A. Children's literature

   B. Preadolescent literature

   C. Adolescent literature

   D. Adult literature

9. Which is NOT a true statement concerning informational texts?
   (Rigorous)

   A. They contain concepts or phenomena.

   B. They could explain history.

   C. They are based on research.

   D. They are presented in a very straightforward, choppy manner.

10. **Which of the following is NOT true of slant rhyme?**
    (Rigorous)

    A. This occurs when a rhyme is not exact

    B. Words are used to evoke meaning by their sounds

    C. The final consonant sounds are the same, but the vowels are different

    D. It occurs frequently in Welsh verse

11. **The literary device of personification is used in which example below?**
    (Average)

    A. "Beg me no beggary by soul or parents, whining dog!"

    B. "Happiness sped through the halls cajoling as it went."

    C. "O wind thy horn, thou proud fellow."

    D. "And that one talent which is death to hide."

12. **All of the following are true about graphic organizers EXCEPT:**
    (Rigorous)

    A. Solidify a visual relationship among various reading and writing ideas

    B. Organize information for an advanced reader

    C. Provide scaffolding for instruction

    D. Activate prior knowledge

13. **The following words are made plural correctly EXCEPT:**
    (Average)

    A. Radios

    B. Bananas

    C. Poppies

    D. Tomatos

14. The following sentences are correct EXCEPT:
    (Rigorous)

    A. One of the boys was playing too rough.

    B. A man and his dog were jogging on the beach.

    C. The House of Representatives has adjourned for the holidays.

    D. Neither Don nor Joyce have missed a day of school this year.

15. All of the following are correctly punctuated EXCEPT:
    (Rigorous)

    A. "The airplane crashed on the runway during takeoff."

    B. I was embarrassed when Mrs. White said, "Your slip is showing!"

    C. "The middle school readers were unprepared to understand Bryant's poem 'Thanatopsis.'"

    D. The hall monitor yelled, "Fire! Fire!"

16. All of the following are true about an expository essay EXCEPT:
    (Average)

    A. Its purpose is to make an experience available through one of the five senses

    B. It is not interested in changing anyone's mind

    C. It exists to give information

    D. It is not trying to get anyone to take a certain action

17. Which is NOT a true statement about narrative writings?
    (Rigorous)

    A. Narratives are interpretive writings

    B. Narratives are organized chronologically

    C. Narratives are based solely on research

    D. Narratives are often presented in the short story format

18. Identify the type of appeal used by Molly Ivins's in this excerpt from her essay "Get a Knife, Get a Dog, But Get Rid of Guns."
    (Rigorous)

    As a civil libertarian, I, of course, support the Second Amendment. And I believe it means exactly what it says:
    "A well regulated militia being necessary to the security of a free state, the right of the people to keep and bear arms shall not be infringed."

    A. Appeal based on writer's credibility

    B. Appeal to logic

    C. Appeal to the emotion

    D. Appeal to the reader

19. "What is the point?" is the first question to be asked when:
    (Average)

    A. Reading a written piece

    B. Listening to a presentation

    C. Writing a composition

    D. All of the above

20. All of the following are true about writing an introduction EXCEPT:
    (Average)

    A. It should be written last

    B. It should lead the audience into the discourse

    C. It is the point of the paper

    A. It can take up a large percentage of the total word count

21. Which of the following is NOT true about a conclusion?
    (Average)

    A. It amplifies the force of the points made in the body of the paper

    B. It apologizes for a deficiency

    C. It arouses appropriate emotions in the reader

    D. It inspires the reader with a favorable opinion of the writer

22. Isaac is mimicking the way his father is writing. He places a piece of paper on the table and holds the pencil in his hand correctly, but he merely draws lines and makes random marks on the paper. What type of writer is he?
    (Average)

    A. Role play writer

    B. Emergent writer

    C. Developing writer

    D. Beginning writer

23. Which of the following sentences is a compound sentence?
    (Average)

    A. Elizabeth took Gracie to the dog park but forgot to bring the leash.
    B. We thoroughly enjoyed our trip during Spring Break and will plan to return next year.
    C. We were given two choices: today or tomorrow.
    D. By the end of the evening, we were thoroughly exhausted; we decided to forego the moonlight walk.

24. Topic sentences, transition words, and appropriate vocabulary are used by writers to:
    (Average)

    A. Meet various purposes

    B. Organize a multi-paragraph essay

    C. Express an attitude on a subject

    D. Explain the presentation of ideas

25. Which of the following should students use to improve coherence of ideas within an argument?
    (Rigorous)

    A. Transitional words or phrases to show relationship of ideas

    B. Conjunctions like "and" to join ideas together

    C. Use direct quotes extensively to improve credibility

    D. Adjectives and adverbs to provide stronger detail

26. **When giving instructions, all of the following are important stylistic elements EXCEPT:**
    (Rigorous)

    A. Present in a serious and friendly tone

    B. Speak clearly and slowly

    C. Note the mood of the audience

    D. Review points of confusion

27. **When speaking on a formal platform, students should do all of the following EXCEPT:**
    (Rigorous)

    A. Use no contractions

    B. Have longer sentences

    C. Connect with the audience

    D. Strictly organize longer segments

28. **To determine an author's purpose a reader must:**
    (Average)

    A. Use his or her own judgment

    B. Verify all the facts

    C. Link the causes to the effects

    D. Rely on common sense

29. **Julia has been hired to work in a school that serves a local public housing project. She is working with kindergarten children and has been asked to focus on shared reading. She selects:**
    (Rigorous)

    A. Chapter books

    B. Riddle books

    C. Alphabet books.

    D. Wordless picture books

30. **Four of Ms. Wolmark's students have lived in other countries. She is particularly pleased to be studying Sumerian proverbs with them as part of the fifth grade unit in analyzing the sayings of other cultures because:**
    (Rigorous)

    A. This gives her a break from teaching, and the children can share sayings from other cultures they and their families have experienced

    B. This validates the experiences and expertise of ELL learners in her classroom

    C. This provides her children from the U.S. with a lens on other cultural values

    D. All of the above

Reading Essays

Sean is five years old and in kindergarten. He is precocious and seems to have a lot of energy throughout the day. Sean has a hard time settling down in the classroom, and the teacher often needs to redirect him in order to have him complete assignments. Sean is struggling in many areas, but currently his lowest area is in writing. Though it is January, Sean still does not seem to be making the appropriate sound symbol connection to make progress with his writing. Sean still needs to be reminded to use a tripod grasp on his pencil and often slips into a fist grip. His drawings are rushed and lack detail but are recognizable. Sean has made some progress with his skills though. At the beginning of the year, he was unable to make any recognizable letters. Now he always makes letters when he is writing; however, there are rarely spaces between the letters. Sean's progress in this area is significantly behind his peers, and you have decided to design an intervention plan to address these concerns.

How would you prioritize the areas where Sean is struggling within your intervention plan and provide justification as to why you would prioritize them in this manner? What instructional activities would you implement as part of the intervention plan? Finally, where else could you seek support and ideas for things to help address Sean's writing skills?

MATH

1. Which of the following statements best characterizes the meaning of "absolute value of x"?
   (Average)

   A. The square root of x

   B. The square of x

   C. The distance on a number line between x and –x

   D. The distance on a number line between 0 and x

2. Which number is equivalent to the following expression?

   $3 \times 10^3 + 9 \times 10^0 + 6 \times 10^{-2} + 8 \times 10^{-3}$

   (Average)

   A. 3,900.68

   B. 3,009.068

   C. 39.68

   D. 309.068

3. Which of the following terms most accurately describes the set of numbers below?

   $\{3, \sqrt{16}, \pi^0, 6, \dfrac{28}{4}\}$

   (Average)

   A. Rationals

   B. Irrationals

   C. Complex

   D. Whole numbers

4. Calculate the value of the following expression.

   $\left(\dfrac{6}{3} + 1 \cdot 5\right)^2 \cdot \left(\dfrac{1}{7}\right) + (3 \cdot 2 - 1)$

   (Average)

   A. 6

   B. 10

   C. 12

   D. 294

5. What is the GCF of 12, 30, 56, and 144?
   (Rigorous)

   A. 2

   B. 3

   C. 5

   D. 7

6. What is the LCM of 6, 7, and 9?
   (Rigorous)

   A. 14

   B. 42

   C. 126

   D. 378

7. In a certain classroom, 32% of the students are male. What is the minimum number of females in the class?
   (Rigorous)

   A. 68

   B. 34

   C. 32

   D. 17

8. The final cost of an item (with sales tax) is $8.35. If the sales tax is 7%, what was the pre-tax price of the item?
   (Average)

   A. $7.80

   B. $8.00

   C. $8.28

   D. $8.93

9. A traveler uses a ruler and finds the distance between two cities to be 3.5 inches. If the legend indicates that 100 miles is the same as an inch, what is the distance in miles between the cities?
   (Average)

   A. 29 miles

   B. 35 miles

   C. 100 miles

   D. 350 miles

10. A burning candle loses ½ inch in height every hour. If the original height of the candle was 6 inches, which of the following equations describes the relationship between the height h of the candle and the number of hours t since it was lit?
(Rigorous)

    A. 2h + t = 12

    B. 2h – t = 12

    C. h = 6 - t

    D. h = 0.5t + 6

11. Three less than four times a number is five times the sum of that number and 6. Which equation could be used to solve this problem?
(Average)

    A. 3 – 4n = 5(n + 6)

    B. 3 – 4n + 5n = 6

    C. 4n – 3 = 5n + 6

    D. 4n – 3 = 5(n + 6)

12. Which set is closed under addition?
(Rigorous)

    A. $\left\{0, \dfrac{1}{2}, \dfrac{1}{4}, \dfrac{1}{8}, \dfrac{1}{16}, \ldots\right\}$

    B. $\{\ldots, -2, -1, 0, 1, 2, \ldots\}$

    C. {–1, 0, 1}

    D. {0, 1, 2, 3, 4, 5}

13. Which property justifies the following manipulation?

    $x^2 - 3y \rightarrow -3y + x^2$

    (Average)

    A. Associative

    B. Commutative

    C. Distributive

    D. None of the above

14. Which set cannot be considered "dense"?
(Rigorous)

    A. Integers

    B. Rationals

    C. Irrationals

    D. Reals

15. Which of the following is an example of a multiplicative inverse?
    (Average)

    A. $x^2 - x^2 = 0$

    B. $(y-3)^0 = 1$

    C. $\dfrac{1}{e^{3z}} e^{3z} = 1$

    D. $f^2 = \dfrac{1}{g}$

16. Two farmers are buying feed for animals. One farmer buys eight bags of grain and six bales of hay for $105, and the other farmer buys three bags of grain and nine bales of hay for $69.75. How much is a bag of grain?
    (Rigorous)

    A. $4.50

    B. $9.75

    C. $14.25

    D. $28.50

17. Which expression best characterizes the shaded area in the graph below?

    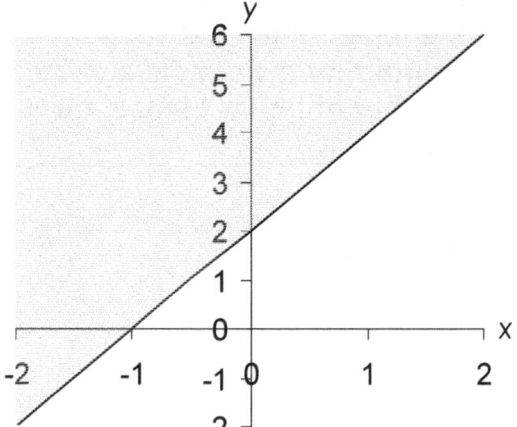

    (Rigorous)

    A. $y \le -x + 2$

    B. $y \ge 2x + 2$

    C. $y = 2x + 2$

    D. $y \ge 2x - 1$

18. Solve for L:

    $$R = r + \dfrac{400(W-L)}{N}$$

    (Rigorous)

    A. $L = W - \dfrac{N}{400}(R-r)$

    B. $L = W + \dfrac{N}{400}(R-r)$

    C. $L = W - \dfrac{400}{N}(R-r)$

    D. $L = \dfrac{NR}{r} - 400W$

19. The formula for the volume of a cylinder is $V = \pi r^2 h$ where r is the radius of the cylinder and h is its height. What is the volume of a cylinder of diameter 2 cm and height 5 cm?
   (Average)

   A. $25\pi \, cm^2$

   B. $5\pi \, cm^2$

   C. $20\pi \, cm^2$

   D. $50\pi \, cm^2$

20. The figure below is an equilateral triangle. Which transformation converts the solid-line figure to the broken-line figure?

   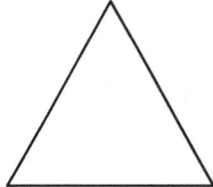

   (Average)

   A. Rotation

   B. Reflection

   C. Glide reflection

   D. Any of the above

21. Which of the following is a net of a cube?
   (Rigorous)

   A.

   B.

   C.

   D.

22. What is the length of the shortest side of a right isosceles triangle if the longest side is 5 centimeters?
   (Rigorous)

   A. 2.24 centimeters

   B. 2.5 centimeters

   C. 3.54 centimeters

   D. Not enough information

23. What is the area of the shaded region below, where the circle has a radius r?

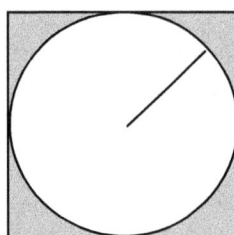

(Average)

A. r^2

B. $(4-\pi)r^2$

C. $(2-\pi)r^2$

D. $4\pi r^2$

24. The figure below is constructed with congruent equilateral triangles each having sides of length 4 units. What is the perimeter of the figure?

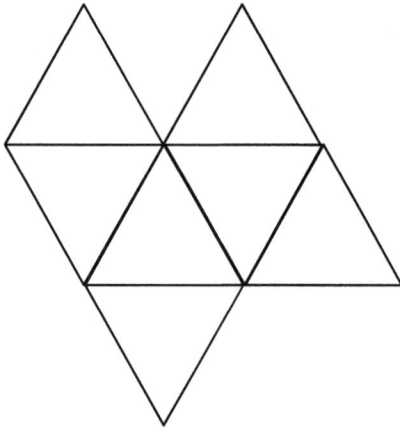

(Average)

A. 9 units

B. 36 units

C. 60 units

D. Not enough information

25. The following stem and leaf plot shows rainfall data in inches over several consecutive days. What is the median value?

0	7
1	3 9
2	1 5 7 8
3	0 3 4 6 6 9
4	3 5 5 7 8
5	0 0 3 5
10	3

    (Average) (

    A. 3.6 in

    B. 3.9 in

    C. 4.3 in

    D. 3.4 in

26. A bag contains four red marbles and six blue marbles. If three selections are made without replacement, what is the probability of choosing three red marbles?
    (Rigorous)

    A. 3/10

    B. 8/125

    C. 1/30

    D. 1/60

27. What is the sample space for the sum of the outcomes for two rolls of a six-sided die?
    (Average)

    A. {1, 2, 3, 4, 5, 6}

    B. {1, 2, 3, 4, 5, 6, 7, 8, 9, 10, 11, 12}

    C. {2, 3, 4, 5, 6, 7, 8, 9, 10, 11, 12}

    D. {7, 8, 9, 10, 11, 12}

28. How many different three-card hands can be drawn from a standard deck of 52 playing cards?
    (Average)

    A. 156

    B. 2,704

    C. 132,600

    D. 140,608

29. How many ways can a card that is either red or a king be selected from a standard deck of 52 playing cards?
    (Average)

    A. 26

    B. 28

    C. 30

    D. 104

30. A set of 5 positive integers has a mean of 7, median of 8 and mode of 9. What is the largest integer in the set?
    (Rigorous)

    A. 12

    B. 8

    C. 9

    D. 10

Math Essays

You have designed an alternative assessment based on a portfolio, observation, and oral presentation for a student with learning disabilities in the area of reading and writing. Your colleague is concerned that this lowers expectations for the student, deprives him of the chance to practice taking the kind of tests he needs to be successful, and sets him further apart from the other students.

Justify your choice of an alternative assessment for the learning-disabled student in place of the traditional tests that other students are taking. How would you respond to your colleague's concerns and reassure her that the assessment you are planning is valid and in the best interests of the student?

SOCIAL SCIENCES

1. Denver is called the "mile-high city" because it is:
   (Average)

   A. Located approximately one mile above the plains of eastern Colorado.

   B. Located exactly one mile above the base of Cheyenne Mountain.

   C. Located approximately one mile above sea level.

   D. The city with the tallest buildings in Colorado.

2. The state of Louisiana is divided into parishes. What type of region do the parishes represent?
   (Rigorous)

   A. Formal region

   B. Functional region

   C. Vernacular region

   D. Human region

3. Which continent is only one country?
   (Average)

   A. Australia.

   B. New Zealand.

   C. The Arctic.

   D. Antarctica.

4. The Southern Hemisphere contains all of which continent?
   (Rigorous)

   A. Africa

   B. Australia

   C. South America

   D. North America

5. Anthropology is:
   (Average)

   A. The profession that made the Leakey family famous

   B. The scientific study of human culture and humanity

   C. Not related to geography at all

   D. Margaret Mead's study of the Samoans

6. In the 1920s, Margaret Mead wrote *Coming of Age in Samoa*, relating her observations about this group's way of life. What of these types of geographical study best describes her method?
   (Rigorous)

   A. Regional

   B. Topical

   C. Physical

   D. Human

7. Which activity is most likely to have a negative environmental impact on an area?
   (Rigorous)

   I. Building a new skyscraper in Manhattan
   II. Strip mining for coal in West Virginia
   III. Digging a new oil well within an existing oilfield in Texas
   IV. Building ten new homes in a 100-acre suburban neighborhood that already contains fifty homes

   A. II and III only

   B. II only

   C. I only

   D. I and IV only

8. Which of the following are two agricultural innovations that began in China?
   (Average)

   A. Using pesticides and fertilizer

   B. Irrigation and cuneiform

   C. Improving the silk industry and inventing gunpowder

   D. Terrace farming and crop rotation

9. Which civilization laid the foundations of geometry?
   (Average)

   A. Egyptian

   B. Greek

   C. Roman

   D. Chinese

10. The international organization established to work for world peace at the end of the Second World War is the:
    (Average)

    A. League of Nations

    B. United Federation of Nations

    C. United Nations

    D. United World League

11. In December, Ms. Griffin asks her students to talk about their holiday traditions. Rebecca explains about lighting the nine candles during Chanukkah, Josh explains about the lighting of the seven candles during Kwanzaa, and Bernard explains about lighting the four candles during Advent. This is an example of:
(Rigorous)

    A. Cross-cultural exchanges

    B. Cultural diffusion

    C. Cultural identity

    D. Cosmopolitanism

12. English and Spanish colonists took what from Native Americans?
(Average)

    A. Land.

    B. Water rights.

    C. Money.

    D. Religious beliefs.

13. Spanish colonies were:
(Average)

    A. Mainly in the northeast

    B. Mainly in the south

    C. Mainly in the Midwest

    D. Mainly in Canada

14. In the events leading up to the American Revolution, which of these methods was effective in dealing with the British taxes?
(Rigorous)

    A. Boycotts

    B. Strikes

    C. Armed conflicts

    D. Resolutions

15. One of the political parties that developed in the early 1790s was led by:
(Rigorous)

    A. Thomas Jefferson.

    B. George Washington.

    C. Aaron Burr.

    D. John Quincy Adams.

16. How did the labor force change after 1830?
(Average)

    A. Employers began using children

    B. Employers began hiring immigrants

    C. Employers began hiring women

    D. Employers began hiring non-immigrant men

17. **Which of these was not a result of World War I in the United States?**
    (Average)

    A. Establishment of new labor laws

    B. Prosperous industrial growth

    C. Formation of the United Nations

    D. Growth of the stock market

18. **Among civilized people:**
    (Average)

    A. Strong government is not necessary.

    B. Systems of control are rudimentary at best.

    C. Government has no sympathy for individuals or for individual happiness.

    D. Governments began to assume more institutional forms.

19. **The U.S. House of Representatives has:**
    (Average)

    A. 100 members

    B. 435 members

    C. Three branches

    D. A president and a vice president

20. **Socialism is:**
    (Rigorous)

    A. A system of government with a legislature

    B. A system where the government is subject to a vote of "no confidence"

    C. A political belief and system in which the state takes a guiding role in the national economy

    D. A system of government with three distinct branches

21. **Which of the following was not a source of conflict in writing the U.S. Constitution?**
    (Average)

    A. Establishing a monarchy

    B. Equalizing power between the small states and the large states

    C. Dealing with slavery

    D. Electing a president

22. In 2002, then-President George W. Bush briefly transferred his presidential power to Vice President Dick Cheney for about an hour while undergoing a colonoscopy. Under what amendment was this covered?
    (Rigorous)

    A. The Nineteenth Amendment

    B. The Twentieth Amendment

    C. The Twenty-second Amendment

    D. The Twenty-fifth Amendment

23. Upon arrest, a person is read a "Miranda warning" which reads, in part, "You have the right to remain silent. Anything you say can and will be used against you in a court of law." Under what amendment in the Bill of Rights is this covered?
    (Rigorous)

    A. The right against unreasonable search and seizures

    B. The right to trial by jury and right to legal council

    C. The right against self-incrimination

    D. The right to jury trial for civil actions

24. The equilibrium price:
    (Rigorous)

    A. Is the price that clears the markets

    B. Is the price in the middle

    C. Identifies a shortage or a surplus

    D. Is an agricultural price support

25. Capital is:
    (Rigorous)

    A. Anyone who sells his or her ability to produce goods and services

    B. The ability of an individual to combine the three inputs with his or her own talents to produce a viable good or service

    C. Anything that is manufactured to be used in the production process

    D. The land itself and everything occurring naturally on it

26. Which of the following countries has historically operated in a market economy?
    (Rigorous)

    A. Great Britain

    B. Cuba

    C. Yugoslavia

    D. India

27. For their research paper on the use of technology in the classroom, students have gathered data that shows a sharp increase in the number of online summer classes over the past five years. What would be the best way for them to depict this information visually?
    (Average)

    A. A line chart

    B. A table

    C. A pie chart

    D. A flow chart

28. An example of something that is not a primary source is:
    (Average)

    A. The published correspondence between Winston Churchill and Franklin D. Roosevelt during World War II

    B. Martin Gilbert's biography of Winston Churchill

    C. The diary of Field Marshal Sir Alan Brooke, the head of the British Army during World War II

    D. Franklin D. Roosevelt's handwritten notes from the World War II era

29. Mr. Phillips is creating a unit to study *To Kill a Mockingbird* and wants to familiarize his high school freshmen with the attitudes and issues of the historical period. Which activity would familiarize students with the attitudes and issues of the Depression-era South?
(Rigorous)

    A. Create a detailed timeline of 15–20 social, cultural, and political events that focus on race relations in the 1930s

    B. Research and report on the life of its author Harper Lee; compare her background with the events in the book

    C. Watch the movie version and note language and dress

    D. Write a research report on the stock market crash of 1929 and its effects

30. Which of the following is not an excellent way to teach students about World War II?
(Rigorous)

    A. To ask a World War II veteran to visit your class and talk to students about the war

    B. To have students read books on World War II

    C. To have students read primary source materials on World War II, such as the text of the Atlantic Charter

    D. To have students watch the movie *Schindler's List*

Social Sciences Essays

You are an elementary school teacher at a Title 1 school. Your school district has been unable to purchase new textbooks for your school in several years. Because of that, the Social Studies textbooks in your classroom are becoming quickly out-dated, and there are no supplemental materials to use for hands-on learning. Along with teaching the content Social Studies standards, you also have to be sure that your students are learning Historical and Social Science Analysis Skills that are often overlooked because of a lack of resources. These skills are not only an important aspect of creating independent thinkers in your classroom, they are also important to making Social Studies come alive for the students, to becoming relevant in their own lives. Being that you only have older Social Studies textbooks at your disposal and no additional resources in the classroom, you have to think "out of the box" to teach these analysis skills to your students.

Historical and Social Science Analysis Skills for grades K–5 include such ideas as:
- Chronological and Spatial Thinking
    - interpreting time lines
    - using terms related to time
    - connections between past and present
    - interpretation of maps and globes, and significance of location
- Research, Evidence, and Point of View
    - differentiation between primary and secondary sources
    - posing relevant questions about events and sources
    - distinguishing between fact and fiction
- Historical Interpretation
    - summarize key events and explain historical context of those events
    - identify human and physical characteristics of places and explain how these are unique to such places
    - identify and interpret multiple causes and effects of events

Given the above information and circumstance, create instructional strategies/activities to teach 2 to 3 of the Historical and Social Science Analysis Skills outlined above. These skills can be taught using any Social Studies content and are for grades K–5 as noted above.

SCIENCE

1. **Which of the following layers comprises the earth's plates?**
   (Easy)

   A. Mesosphere

   B. Troposphere

   C. Asthensophere

   D. Lithosphere

2. **The Himalayas, a folded mountain range, have formed at a:**
   (Average)

   A. Divergent plate boundary

   B. A continental-oceanic convergent plate boundary

   C. An oceanic-oceanic convergent plate boundary

   D. A continental-continental convergent plate boundary

3. **What conditions are required to create coarse-grained igneous rocks?**
   (Average)

   A. High temperature and pressure

   B. Slowly cooling magma

   C. Quickly cooling lava

   D. Evaporation and cementation

4. **Which of the following describes the law of superposition?**
   (Easy)

   A. The present is the key to the past

   B. The oldest rocks in a rock unit are found on the top of the rock column

   C. The oldest rocks in a rock unit are found on the bottom of the rock column

   D. Faults that cut across rock units are younger than the units they cut across

5. **How are igneous, metamorphic, and sedimentary rocks classified?**
   (Average)

   A. The chemical composition of the rocks

   B. When the rocks were formed

   C. How the rocks were formed

   D. The location of the rocks within the Earth's crust

6. In which period did land animals first appear?
   (Easy)

   A. 350 to 135 million years ago

   B. Devonian

   C. Paleozoic

   D. Cretaceous

7. Which era had dinosaurs in it?
   (Easy)

   A. Cenozoic

   B. Mesozoic

   C. Triassic

   D. Paleozoic

8. Which of the following objects in the universe is the largest?
   (Average)

   A. Pulsars

   B. Quasars

   C. Black holes

   D. Nebulas

9. Why is the northern winter slightly warmer than the southern winter?
   (Average)

   A. Because the perihelion occurs in January

   B. Because of global warming

   C. Because there is more water in the southern hemisphere

   D. Because Earth rotates on an axis that is not perpendicular to the plane of rotation.

10. What are ribosomes?
    (Easy)

    A. Contain digestive enzymes that break down food

    B. Where proteins are synthesized

    C. Make ATP

    D. Hold stored food

11. The role of rough endoplasmic reticulum is:
    (Easy)

    A. Metabolic functions

    B. Produce lipids

    C. Produce enzymes

    D. Protein synthesis

12. **What is the purpose of sexual reproduction?**
    (Rigorous)

    A. Produce more organisms

    B. Produce organisms that are genetically diverse

    C. Give organisms the protection of male and female parents

    D. Increase social cooperation between organisms

13. **In mitotic cell division, at what stage do the chromosomes line up in the cell?**
    (Average)

    A. Interphase

    B. Anaphase

    C. Prophase

    D. Metaphase

14. **Oogenesis is the formation of:**
    (Easy)

    A. Eggs

    B. Sperm

    C. Pollen

    D. Cytoplasm

15. **According to natural selection:**
    (Easy)

    A. Individuals within a population are identical

    B. Those with better traits have less offspring

    C. Successive generations will possess better traits

    D. Single individuals evolve to fit their surroundings

16. **Chemicals released by an organism as way of communicating are called:**
    (Easy)

    A. Pheromones

    B. Synapses

    C. Chemoreceptors

    D. Thermoreceptors

17. **Which of the following is not a kingdom in the classification of living organisms?**
    (Average)

    A. Plants

    B. Fungi

    C. Viruses

    D. Bacteria

18. Which property do plants have that fungi do not have?
    (Average)

    A. Sexual reproduction

    B. Photosynthesis

    C. Digestion

    D. Locomotion

19. Which term describes the relationship between barnacles and whales?
    (Rigorous)

    A. Commensalism

    B. Parasitism

    C. Competition

    D. Mutualism

20. Which of the following describes the transformation of liquid water to ice?
    (Average)

    A. Chemical change

    B. Physical change

    C. Thermodynamic change

    D. Non-chemical molecular change

21. Will Lithium gain or lose an electron when forming an ion? How many electrons will it gain or lose?
    (Average)

    A. Gain 1

    B. Gain 2

    C. Lose 1

    D. Lose 2

22. On which of the following does the force of friction between a metal stool and a wooden floor <u>not</u> depend?
    (Rigorous)

    A. The speed of the chair

    B. Whether the stool has three legs or four

    C. The type of metal

    D. The smoothness of the floor

23. Which of the following laws implies that the force on an object comes from another object?
    (Average)

    A. Newton's first law of motion

    B. Newton's second law of motion

    C. Newton's third law of motion

    D. Coulomb's law

24. Which of the following quantities has the units of calories per degree?
    (Easy)

    A. Heat capacity

    B. Specific heat

    C. Heat equivalent

    D. Heat transfer

25. How does a steam radiator deliver heat energy to a room?
    (Rigorous)

    A. Radiation

    B. Conduction

    C. Convection

    D. Contact

26. What kind of chemical reaction is photosynthesis?
    (Rigorous)

    A. Fusion

    B. Exothermic

    C. Endothermic

    D. Could be exothermic or endothermic

27. A controlled experiment with tomato plants was conducted to see if the amount of water given to the plants affected the number of tomatoes grown. One plant was given 1 gallon of water, another 2 gallons, another 3 gallons, etc. The number of tomatoes produced for each plant was measured. What was the controlled variable?
    (Average)

    A. Type of plant

    B. Amount of water

    C. Number of tomatoes

    D. Amount of fertilizer

28. Which of the following should be limited in a balanced diet?
    (Easy)

    A. Carbohydrates

    B. Fats and oils

    C. Proteins

    D. Vitamins

29. Which of the following statements about scientific knowledge best explains what scientific knowledge is:
    (Average)

    A. Scientific knowledge is based on experiments
    B. Science knowledge is empirical
    C. Scientific knowledge is tentative
    D. Scientific knowledge is based on reason

30. An experiment is performed to determine the effects of acid rain on plant life. Which of the following would be the variable?
    (Average)

    A. The type of plant

    B. The amount of light

    C. The pH of the water

    D. The amount of water

Science Essays

A mechanical wave is a disturbance in a medium in which energy is propagated but not bulk matter. Waves can be transverse or longitudinal. A wave has frequency, amplitude, and wavelength. The speed of a wave is determined by the medium.

What would be the instructional objective, lesson motivation, and student activity in a lesson about waves?

Elementary Education
Post-Test Sample Questions with Rationales

READING

1. To make an inference a reader must:
   (Average)

   A. Make a logical guess as to the next event.

   B. Find a line of reasoning on which to rely.

   C. Make a decision based on an observation.

   D. Use prior knowledge and apply it to the current situation.

Answer: D. Use prior knowledge and apply it to the current situation.
Prior knowledge applied to the situation at hand is essential in making a valid inference. Because choices A–C do not involve prior knowledge, they are not correct ways to make an inference.

2. Which of the following is NOT utilized by a reader when trying to comprehend the meaning behind the literal text?
   (Rigorous)

   A. Pictures and graphics in the text

   B. Background knowledge about a topic

   C. Knowledge of different types of text structure

   D. Context clues

Answer: A. Pictures and graphics in the text
While pictures and graphics can be helpful, good readers are trying to extract meaning from the text itself by comparing new information to background knowledge, using knowledge of a type of text to build expectations, and making use of context clues to help identify unknown words.

3. **Phonological awareness includes all of the following skills except:**
   (Average)

   A. Rhyming and syllabification

   B. Blending sounds into words

   C. Understanding the meaning of the root word

   D. Removing initial sounds and substituting others

Answer: C. understanding the meaning of the root word
Phonological awareness involves the recognition that spoken words are composed of a set of smaller units such as onsets and rhymes, syllables, and sounds.

4. **Asking a child if what he or she has read makes sense to him or her, is prompting the child to use:**
   (Average)

   A. Phonics cues

   B. Syntactic cues

   C. Semantic cues

   D. Prior knowledge

Answer: C. Semantic cues
Children use their prior knowledge, sense of the story, and pictures to support their predicting and confirming the meaning of the text.

5. Which of the following indicates that a student is a fluent reader?
   (Rigorous)

   A. Reads texts with expression or prosody

   B. Reads word-to-word and haltingly

   C. Must intentionally decode a majority of the words

   D. In a writing assignment, sentences are poorly-organized, structurally

Answer: A. Reads texts with expression or prosody.
The teacher should listen to the children read aloud, but there are also clues to reading levels in their writing.

6. If a student has a poor vocabulary the teacher should recommend that:
   (Rigorous)

   A. The student read newspapers, magazines, and books on a regular basis

   B. The student enroll in a Latin class

   C. The student writes the words repetitively after looking them up in the dictionary

   D. The student use a thesaurus to locate synonyms and incorporate them into his/her vocabulary

Answer: A. The student read newspapers, magazines, and books on a regular basis.
It is up to the teacher to help the student choose reading material, but the student must be able to choose where s/he will search for the reading pleasure indispensable for enriching vocabulary.

7. **To decode is to:**
   (Average)

   A. Construct meaning

   B. Sound out a printed sequence of letters

   C. Use a special code to decipher a message

   D. None of the above

Answer: B. Sound out a printed sequence of letters.
To decode means to change communication signals into messages. Reading comprehension requires that the reader learn the code within which a message is written and be able to decode it to get the message.

8. **John Bunyan, Coleridge, Shakespeare, Homer, and Chaucer all contributed to what genre of literature?**
   (Average)

   A. Children's literature

   B. Preadolescent literature

   C. Adolescent literature

   D. Adult literature

Answer: D. Adult literature
These five authors contributed to the adult literature genre as they were authoring titles before children's and preadolescent/adolescent literature became recognized as separate genres that authors purposefully contributed towards.

9. Which is NOT a true statement concerning informational texts?
(Rigorous)

    A.   They contain concepts or phenomena

    B.   They could explain history

    C.   They are based on research

    D.   They are presented in a very straightforward, choppy manner

Answer: D. They are presented in a very straightforward, choppy manner
Informational texts are types of books that explain concepts or phenomena like history or the idea of photosynthesis. Informational texts are usually based on research. Texts that are presented in a very straightforward or choppy manner are newspaper articles.

10. Which of the following is NOT true of slant rhyme?
(Rigorous)

    A.   This occurs when a rhyme is not exact

    B.   Words are used to evoke meaning by their sounds

    C.   The final consonant sounds are the same, but the vowels are different

    D.   It occurs frequently in Welsh verse

Answer: B. Words are used to evoke meaning by their sounds
Slant rhyme occurs when a rhyme is not exact because the final consonant sounds may be the same while the vowel sounds are different. Examples include: "green" and "gone" or "that" and "hit." This type of device occurs frequently in Welsh verse as well as in Irish and Icelandic verse. Poets who use words to evoke meaning by their sounds are using onomatopoeia.

11. **The literary device of personification is used in which example below?**
    (Average)

    A. "Beg me no beggary by soul or parents, whining dog!"

    B. "Happiness sped through the halls cajoling as it went."

    C. "O wind thy horn, thou proud fellow."

    D. "And that one talent which is death to hide."

Answer: B. "Happiness sped through the halls cajoling as it went."
The correct answer is B. Personification is defined as giving human characteristics to inanimate objects or concepts. It can be thought of as a sub-category of metaphor. Happiness, an abstract concept, is "speeding through the halls" and "cajoling," both of which are human behaviors, so happiness is being compared to a human being. Choice A is figurative and metaphorical but not a personification. Choice C is, again, figurative and metaphorical but not a personification. The speaker is, perhaps, telling someone that they are bragging, or "blowing their own horn." Choice D is also figurative and metaphorical but not personification. Hiding a particular talent is being compared to risking death.

12. **All of the following are true about graphic organizers EXCEPT:**
    (Rigorous)

    A. Solidify a visual relationship among various reading and writing ideas

    B. Organize information for an advanced reader

    C. Provide scaffolding for instruction

    D. Activate prior knowledge

Answer: B. Organize information for an advanced reader.
A graphic organizer is a tool that students can use to help them visualize ideas in a text. They are also a helpful scaffolding tool as they help students activate their prior knowledge on the topic at hand. Choice B is incorrect because graphic organizers are relevant tools for young and/or basic readers and are not just for the advanced or independent.

13. **The following words are made plural correctly EXCEPT:**
    (Average)

    A.   Radios

    B.   Bananas

    C.   Poppies

    D.   Tomatos

Answer: D. Tomatos
Words that end in *o* with a consonant before it require adding an *es* for the plural form. *Radio* does not have a consonant before the *o* and therefore only takes the *s* ending to avoid three vowels in a row.

14. **The following sentences are correct EXCEPT:**
    (Rigorous)

    A.   One of the boys was playing too rough.

    B.   A man and his dog were jogging on the beach.

    C.   The House of Representatives has adjourned for the holidays.

    D.   Neither Don nor Joyce have missed a day of school this year.

Answer: D. Neither Don nor Joyce have missed a day of school this year.
A verb should always agree in number with its subject. Making them agree requires the ability to locate the subject of a sentence. In choice A the subject, one, is singular and requires a singular verb. In choice B the subject, man and dog, is plural and requires a plural verb, In choice C the subject, House of Representatives, is collectively singular and requires a singular verb. In choice D the subject, Don and Joyce, are both singular and connected by nor which requires the use of a singular verb, and "have" is plural and therefore incorrect.

15. **All of the following are correctly punctuated EXCEPT:**
    (Rigorous)

    A. "The airplane crashed on the runway during takeoff."

    B. I was embarrassed when Mrs. White said, "Your slip is showing!"

    C. "The middle school readers were unprepared to understand Bryant's poem 'Thanatopsis.'"

    D. The hall monitor yelled, "Fire! Fire!"

Answer: B. I was embarrassed when Mrs. White said, "Your slip is showing!"
Choice B is incorrectly punctuated because in sentences that are exclamatory, the exclamation point should be positioned outside the closing quotation marks if the quote itself is a statement, command, or cited title. The exclamation point is correctly positioned in choice D because the sentence is declarative, but the quotation is an exclamation.

16. **All of the following are true about an expository essay EXCEPT:**
    (Average)

    A. Its purpose is to make an experience available through one of the five senses

    B. It is not interested in changing anyone's mind

    C. It exists to give information

    D. It is not trying to get anyone to take a certain action

Answer: A. Its purpose is to make an experience available through one of the five senses
The expository essay's purpose is to inform and not persuade or describe. Choice A is the purpose of a descriptive essay.

17. **Which is NOT a true statement about narrative writings?**
    (Rigorous)

    A. Narratives are interpretive writings

    B. Narratives are organized chronologically

    C. Narratives are based solely on research

    D. Narratives are often presented in the short story format

Answer: C. Narratives are based solely on research
Narratives are not based solely on research. While an author may complete research to help them write a historically or culturally based narrative, they will use personal interpretation and a short story format to tell the story. Neither of those elements would exist in a piece that is solely based on research.

18. **Identify the type of appeal used by Molly Ivins's in this excerpt from her essay "Get a Knife, Get a Dog, But Get Rid of Guns."**
    (Rigorous)

    As a civil libertarian, I, of course, support the Second Amendment. And I believe it means exactly what it says:
    "A well regulated militia being necessary to the security of a free state, the right of the people to keep and bear arms shall not be infringed."

    A. Appeal based on writer's credibility

    B. Appeal to logic

    C. Appeal to the emotion

    D. Appeal to the reader

Answer: A. Appeal based on writer's credibility
By announcing that she is a civil libertarian and that she supports the Second Amendment, the author is establishing her credibility. At this point, Ivins has not provided reasons or appealed to the emotion, nor has she addressed the reader.

19. "What is the point?" is the first question to be asked when: (Average

    A.   Reading a written piece

    B.   Listening to a presentation

    C.   Writing a composition

    D.   All of the above

Answer: D. All of the above
When reading, listening, or writing one should first ask, "What is the point?" The answer will be in the thesis. If a piece doesn't make a point, the reader/listener/viewer is likely to be confused or feel that it was not worth the effort.

20. All of the following are true about writing an introduction EXCEPT: (Average)

    A.   It should be written last

    B.   It should lead the audience into the discourse

    C.   It is the point of the paper

    D.   It can take up a large percentage of the total word count

Answer: C. It is the point of the paper
The thesis is the point of the paper not the introduction. The rest of the choices are true about an introduction.

21. Which of the following is NOT true about a conclusion?
    (Average)

    A. It amplifies the force of the points made in the body of the paper

    B. It apologizes for a deficiency

    C. It arouses appropriate emotions in the reader

    D. It inspires the reader with a favorable opinion of the writer

Answer: B. It apologizes for a deficiency
Apologizing for a deficiency is a tactic for introducing a topic in an introduction. The other choices are true of a conclusion.

22. Isaac is mimicking the way his father is writing. He places a piece of paper on the table and holds the pencil in his hand correctly, but he merely draws lines and makes random marks on the paper. What type of writer is he?
    (Average)

    A. Role play writer

    B. Emergent writer

    C. Developing writer

    D. Beginning writer

Answer: C. Role play writer.
A role play writer uses writing-like behavior but has no phonetic association. He is aware of print but scribbles at this point. .

23. **Which of the following sentences is a compound sentence?**
    (Average)

    A. Elizabeth took Gracie to the dog park but forgot to bring the leash.

    B. We thoroughly enjoyed our trip during Spring Break and will plan to return next year.

    C. We were given two choices: today or tomorrow.

    D. By the end of the evening, we were thoroughly exhausted; we decided to forego the moonlight walk.

Answer: D. By the end of the evening, we were thoroughly exhausted; we decided to forego the moonlight walk.
A compound sentence is two independent clauses joined by a coordinating conjunction or a semicolon. The sentences in choices A, B, and C have coordinating conjunctions but they do not connect two clauses. Sentences A and B have compound verb phrases. Sentence C has a compound object.

24. **Topic sentences, transition words, and appropriate vocabulary are used by writers to:**
    (Average)

    A. Meet various purposes

    B. Organize a multi-paragraph essay

    C. Express an attitude on a subject

    D. Explain the presentation of ideas

Answer: B. Organize a multi-paragraph essay
Correctly organizing an essay allows a writer to clearly communicate their ideas. To organize, a writer needs topic sentences, transition words, and appropriate vocabulary. Meeting a purpose, expressing an attitude, and explaining ideas are all done by an author in a piece of writing, but they are separate elements.

25. **Which of the following should students use to improve coherence of ideas within an argument?**
    (Rigorous)

    A. Transitional words or phrases to show relationship of ideas

    B. Conjunctions like "and" to join ideas together

    C. Use direct quotes extensively to improve credibility

    D. Adjectives and adverbs to provide stronger detail

Answer: A. Transitional words or phrases to show relationship of ideas
Transitional words and phrases are two-way indicators that connect the previous idea to the following idea. Sophisticated writers use transitional devices to clarify text (for example), to show contrast (despite), to show sequence (first, next), to show cause (because).

26. **When giving instructions, all of the following are important stylistic elements EXCEPT:**
    (Rigorous)

    A. Present in a serious and friendly tone.

    B. Speak clearly and slowly.

    C. Note the mood of the audience.

    D. Review points of confusion.

Answer: A. Present in a serious and friendly tone.
Not all types of public speaking will have the same type of speaking style. When giving instructions, it is important to speak clearly and slowly, note the mood of the audience, and review if there is confusion. Presenting in a serious and friendly tone won't help the instructions be any more clear and is an important stylistic element of giving an oral presentation.

27. **When speaking on a formal platform, students should do all of the following EXCEPT:**
    (Rigorous)

    A. Use no contractions

    B. Have longer sentences

    C. Connect with the audience

    D. Strictly organize longer segments

Answer: C. Connect with the audience
When speaking formally, students should use fewer or no contractions, have longer sentences, and be more organized during longer segments of the speech. While connecting with the audience may seem beneficial, the personal antidotes or humorous pieces required to do that are not appropriate in a formal setting.

28. **To determine an author's purpose a reader must:**
    (Average)

    A. Use his or her own judgment.

    B. Verify all the facts.

    C. Link the causes to the effects.

    D. Rely on common sense.

Answer: A. Use his or her own judgment.
An author may have more than one purpose in writing. There are no tricks or rules to follow, and the reader must use his or her own judgment to determine the author's purpose for writing. Verifying all the facts, linking causes to effects, and relying on common sense can all help a reader in judging the author's purpose, but none are solely responsible.

29. **Julia has been hired to work in a school that serves a local public housing project. She is working with kindergarten children and has been asked to focus on shared reading. She selects:**
(Rigorous)

    A.   Chapter books

    B.   Riddle books

    C.   Alphabet books

    D.   Wordless picture books

Answer: D   Wordless picture books
Wordless picture books allow students to derive the story events from the illustrations and prevent stumbling over words they are unable to identify.

30. **Four of Ms. Wolmark's students have lived in other countries. She is particularly pleased to be studying Sumerian proverbs with them as part of the fifth grade unit in analyzing the sayings of other cultures because:**
(Rigorous)

    A.   This gives her a break from teaching, and the children can share sayings from other cultures they and their families have experienced
    B.   This validates the experiences and expertise of ELL learners in her classroom
    C.   This provides her children from the U.S. with a lens on other cultural values
    D.   All of the above

Answer: D. All of the above
It is recommended that all teachers of reading and particularly those who are working with ELL students use meaningful, student centered, and culturally customized activities. These activities may include: language games, word walls, and poems. Some of these activities might, if possible, be initiated in the child's first language and then reiterated in English.

Answer Key: Reading

1. D	16. A
2. A	17. C
3. C	18. A
4. C	19. D
5. A	20. C
6. A	21. B
7. B	22. C
8. D	23. D
9. D	24. B
10. B	25. A
11. B	26. A
12. B	27. C
13. D	28. A
14. D	29. D
15. B	30. D

Rigor Table: Reading

	Easy 0%	Average 50%	Rigorous 50%
Questions		1, 3, 4, 7, 8, 11, 13, 16, 19, 20, 21, 22, 23, 24, 28	2, 5, 6, 9, 10, 12, 14, 15, 17, 18, 25, 26, 27, 29, 30

Reading Essays

Sean is five years old and in kindergarten. He is precocious and seems to have a lot of energy throughout the day. Sean has a hard time settling down in the classroom, and the teacher often needs to redirect him in order to have him complete assignments. Sean is struggling in many areas, but currently his lowest area is in writing. Though it is January, Sean still does not seem to be making the appropriate sound symbol connection to make progress with his writing. Sean still needs to be reminded to use a tripod grasp on his pencil and often slips into a fist grip. His drawings are rushed and lack detail but are recognizable. Sean has made some progress with his skills though. At the beginning of the year, he was unable to make any recognizable letters. Now he always makes letters when he is writing; however, there are rarely spaces between the letters. Sean's progress in this area is significantly behind his peers, and you have decided to design an intervention plan to address these concerns.

How would you prioritize the areas where Sean is struggling within your intervention plan and provide justification as to why you would prioritize them in this manner? What instructional activities would you implement as part of the intervention plan? Finally, where else could you seek support and ideas for things to help address Sean's writing skills?

Sample Good Response

The first step in creating any intervention plan for a student is to prioritize the areas in which the student is struggling. In Sean's case, there are many different areas where he is struggling. The first one I would address is the sound symbol connection. I would choose this area because in order for any student to be able to complete any type of writing assignment, they need to have an understanding of what sounds letters make. If Sean does not know that the letter b makes the /b/ sound, then when he is sounding out words and comes across the /b/ sound, he will have no idea what symbol to write for that sound. In order, to address this skill, I would incorporate a great deal of phonemic awareness activities to develop Sean's sound symbol awareness. If I was unable to make progress or lacking in appropriate activities, I could seek support from a colleague or a reading specialist to obtain further ideas.

After this, I would work on spacing. In this area, I would use a tool that Sean could use to help him create spaces in his writing. A clothespin works well and can be given a face with a marker to be called a spaceman. The spaceman can be used by Sean to lie down on his paper after every word he writes so that he has an appropriate sized space between words. Eventually, this tool can be weaned away from Sean as he learns to create appropriate spaces without the tool.

Finally, I would address Sean's lack of the use of a tripod grasp by providing him with broken crayons to use multiple times throughout the day. When children use small pieces of crayons, the hands automatically form the appropriate grasp in order to hold such a small writing tool. When he has to write, there are special pencil grips or pencils that encourage the appropriate grasp as well. I would consult with the schools occupational therapist assigned to my school for further ideas and suggestions to improve Sean's fine motor schools.

Sample Poor Response

I would start with talking to Sean's parents about his inability to focus. If Sean could pay better attention, he would be able to write more appropriately. Having a parent teacher conference would help the parents to see how Sean is struggling within the classroom and seek out help from doctors to address his attention issues.

Then I would work on spelling activities with him. By giving Sean words to learn and memorize, he will be able to transfer these to his writing. If he was able to already know how to spell words, he will be more able to write things correctly. This will help him to be able to write more like his peers.

Finally, I would give him sentences with one blank to fill in, rather than letting him come up with his own ideas. If he only has to focus on one idea, he will be more likely to be able to be successful than having to think of the entire sentence.

MATH

1. Which of the following statements best characterizes the meaning of "absolute value of x"?
(Average)

   A. The square root of x

   B. The square of x

   C. The distance on a number line between x and –x

   D. The distance on a number line between 0 and x

Answer: D. The distance on a number line between 0 and x
The absolute value of a number x is best described as the distance on a number line between 0 and x, regardless of whether x is positive or negative. Note that the following expression is valid for x ≥ 0:

$$|x| = |-x|$$

2. Which number is equivalent to the following expression?

$$3 \times 10^3 + 9 \times 10^0 + 6 \times 10^{-2} + 8 \times 10^{-3}$$

   (Average)

   A. 3,900.68

   B. 3,009.068

   C. 39.68

   D. 309.068

Answer: B. 3,009.068
Each product represents a digit in a specific place in the decimal. We can find the value of the number by calculating the products and adding, or by simply noting that the 3 is in the thousands place, the 9 is in the ones place, the 6 is in the hundredths place, and the 8 is in the thousandths place. Zeroes are in all other places.

$$3 \times 10^3 + 9 \times 10^0 + 6 \times 10^{-2} + 8 \times 10^{-3} = 3,009.068$$

3. **Which of the following terms most accurately describes the set of numbers below?**

$$\{3, \sqrt{16}, \pi^0, 6, \frac{28}{4}\}$$

(Average)

    A.   Rationals

    B.   Irrationals

    C.   Complex

    D.   Whole numbers

Answer: D. Whole numbers
Let's simplify the set of numbers as follows.

    $\{3, 4, 1, 6, 7\}$

Note that this set of numbers can be described as real numbers, rationals, integers, and whole numbers, but they are *best* described as whole numbers.

4. Calculate the value of the following expression.

$$\left(\frac{6}{3}+1\cdot 5\right)^2 \cdot \left(\frac{1}{7}\right)+(3\cdot 2-1)$$

(Average)

- A. 6
- B. 10
- C. 12
- D. 294

Answer: C. 12

Apply the correct order of operations to get the correct result: first, calculate all terms in parentheses, followed by exponents, division and multiplication, and addition and subtraction (in that order).

$$(2+5)^2 \cdot \left(\frac{1}{7}\right)+(6-1)=7^2 \cdot \frac{1}{7}+5=49\cdot \frac{1}{7}+5=7+5=12$$

5. **What is the GCF of 12, 30, 56, and 144?**
   (Rigorous)

   A.   2

   B.   3

   C.   5

   D.   7

Answer: A. 2
One way to determine the greatest common factor (GCF) is to list the factors for each number. Although this can be tedious, it is a relatively sure method of determining the GCF. Note that you need not determine any factors larger than the smallest number in the list (12, in this case)—12 doesn't have any factors greater than 12.

12:   2, 3, 4, 6, 12
30:   2, 3, 5, 6, 10
56:   2, 4, 7, 8
144: 2, 3, 4, 6, 8, 9, 12

By inspection of these lists, we see that 2 is the greatest common factor.

6.   What is the LCM of 6, 7, and 9?
   (Rigorous)

   A.   14

   B.   42

   C.   126

   D.   378

Answer: C. 126
The least common multiple (LCM) is smallest number for which the numbers given above are factors. We can approach this problem in one of several ways. One possibility is to list multiples of each number until we come across a multiple common to all three, or we can determine the prime factors of each number and use those to determine an LCM.

6:   6, 12, 18, 24, 30, 36, 42, 48…
7:   7, 14, 21, 28, 35, 42, 49…
9:   9, 18, 27, 36, 45, 54, 63, 72…

As yet, the lists above do not show any common multiples. Let's try multiplying the prime factors of each number until we find a common multiple.

$6 = 2 \cdot 3$ $\qquad\qquad 7 = 7 \qquad\qquad 9 = 3 \cdot 3$

$2 \cdot 3 \cdot 7 = 42$ (not a common multiple)
$2 \cdot 3 \cdot 3 \cdot 7 = 126$ (LCM)

If you continued the lists of multiples, which was our first attempt, you will eventually find that 126 is the first (and least) common multiple.

7. In a certain classroom, 32% of the students are male. What is the minimum number of females in the class?
(Rigorous)

    A.   68

    B.   34

    C.   32

    D.   17

Answer: D. 17
Obviously, the classroom can only have a whole number of students. Let's call this number x. We know that $0.32x$ is the number of males; the number of females must then be $0.68x$. If f is the number of females, then

$$f = \frac{68}{100} x$$

Since f is a whole number, we must find the smallest value of x for which $68x$ is divisible by 100. But if we simplify the fraction, then

$$f = \frac{17}{25} x$$

Thus, we see that $x = 25$ is a possibility. Because 17 is a prime number and x must be a whole number, $x = 25$ is the smallest possible value. Then,

$$f = \frac{17}{25}(25) = 17$$

The classroom must therefore have a minimum of 17 female students.

8. The final cost of an item (with sales tax) is $8.35. If the sales tax is 7%, what was the pre-tax price of the item?
   (Average)

   A. $7.80

   B. $8.00

   C. $8.28

   D. $8.93

Answer: A. $7.80
We can solve this problem by constructing a proportionality expression. Let's call the pre-tax price of the item *x*; then, if we add 7% of *x* to this price, we get a final cost of $8.35.

$x + 0.07x = \$8.35$
$1.07x = \$8.35$
$x = \dfrac{\$8.35}{1.07} = \$7.80$

Thus, the initial price of the item was $7.80 (answer A). You can also determine this answer by multiplying each option by 1.07; the correct answer is the one that yields a product of $8.35.

9. A traveler uses a ruler and finds the distance between two cities to be 3.5 inches. If the legend indicates that 100 miles is the same as an inch, what is the distance in miles between the cities?
(Average)

   A. 29 miles

   B. 35 miles

   C. 100 miles

   D. 350 miles

Answer: D. 350 miles
Construct a proportion relating inches to miles. Let the unknown distance in miles be *d*.

$$\frac{100 \text{ miles}}{1 \text{ inch}} = \frac{d}{3.5 \text{ inches}}$$

Cross multiply to find the value of *d*.

$$d = 3.5 \text{ inches} \cdot \frac{100 \text{ miles}}{1 \text{ inch}} = 350 \text{ miles}$$

10. A burning candle loses ½ inch in height every hour. If the original height of the candle was 6 inches, which of the following equations describes the relationship between the height h of the candle and the number of hours t since it was lit?
(Average)

    A. 2h + t = 12

    B. 2h − t = 12

    C. h = 6 - t

    D. h = 0.5t + 6

Answer: A. 2h + t = 12
Since the height of the candle is falling, the slope = -1/2. Thus, the equation in the slope-intercept form is h = -(1/2)t + 6 since h = 6 for t = 0. Multiplying both sides of the equation by 2, we get 2h = -t + 12 or 2h + t = 12.

11. **Three less than four times a number is five times the sum of that number and 6. Which equation could be used to solve this problem?**
    (Average)

    A. $3 - 4n = 5(n + 6)$

    B. $3 - 4n + 5n = 6$

    C. $4n - 3 = 5n + 6$

    D. $4n - 3 = 5(n + 6)$

Answer: D. $4n - 3 = 5(n + 6)$
Be sure to enclose the sum of the number and 6 in parentheses.

12. **Which set is closed under addition?**
    (Rigorous)

    A. $\{0, \frac{1}{2}, \frac{1}{4}, \frac{1}{8}, \frac{1}{16}, \ldots\}$

    B. $\{\ldots, -2, -1, 0, 1, 2, \ldots\}$

    C. $\{-1, 0, 1\}$

    D. $\{0, 1, 2, 3, 4, 5\}$

Answer: B. $\{\ldots, -2, -1, 0, 1, 2, \ldots\}$
For a set to be closed under a particular operation, then that operation performed on any two members of the set must yield a result that is also a member of the set. Thus, we can easily show that choices A, C, and D are not closed under addition by counterexamples. For answer A, $\frac{1}{2} + \frac{1}{2} = 1$, but 1 is not a member of the set. Likewise, for answer C, 1 + 1 = 2, but 2 is not a member of the set. The same type of reasoning can be applied to choice D. For choice B (the set of integers), however, we know that the sum of any two integers is another integer. Thus, the set of numbers in B is closed under addition.

13. Which property justifies the following manipulation?

    $x^2 - 3y \to -3y + x^2$

    (Average)

    A. Associative

    B. Commutative

    C. Distributive

    D. None of the above

Answer: B. Commutative
The commutative property tells us that $a + b = b + a$; thus, the manipulation of the algebraic expression in the problem statement can be justified by the commutative property.

14. Which set cannot be considered "dense"?
    (Rigorous)

    A. Integers

    B. Rationals

    C. Irrationals

    D. Reals

Answer: A. Integers
A set of numbers is considered dense if between any two arbitrary values from the set, there exists another value from the set that lies between these two values. For instance, between 1 and 3 is the number 2. For integers, however, there is no integer between 1 and 2, for example (or between any two consecutive integers). Thus, the correct answer is choice A. For the other sets (rationals, irrationals, and reals), there is always a value between any two arbitrary values from those sets.

15. **Which of the following is an example of a multiplicative inverse?**
    (Average)

    A. $x^2 - x^2 = 0$

    B. $(y-3)^0 = 1$

    C. $\dfrac{1}{e^{3z}} e^{3z} = 1$

    D. $f^2 = \dfrac{1}{g}$

Answer: C. $\dfrac{1}{e^{3z}} e^{3z} = 1$

A multiplicative inverse has the form:

$$a \cdot \dfrac{1}{a} = 1$$

Thus, answer C best fits this definition.

16. Two farmers are buying feed for animals. One farmer buys eight bags of grain and six bales of hay for $105, and the other farmer buys three bags of grain and nine bales of hay for $69.75. How much is a bag of grain?
    (Rigorous)

    A. $4.50

    B. $9.75

    C. $14.25

    D. $28.50

Answer: B. $9.75
Let x be the price of a bag of grain, and let y be the price of a bale of hay. We can then write two equations based on the information provided in the problem.

Farmer 1: $8x + 6y = \$105$
Farmer 2: $3x + 9y = \$69.75$

We want to find x, the price of a bag of grain. One approach to solving this problem is to solve either the first or second equation for y and then substitute the result into the other equation and solve for x. Another approach involves subtraction. Let's multiply both sides of the second equation by 2/3.

$$\frac{2}{3}(3x + 9y = \$69.75)$$
$2x + 6y = \$46.50$

Now, subtract this from the first equation.

$$\begin{array}{r} 8x + 6y = \$105 \\ -\ 2x + 6y = \$46.50 \\ \hline 6x \quad\quad = \$58.5 \end{array}$$

Solving for x yields the solution.

$x = \$9.75$

17. Which expression best characterizes the shaded area in the graph below?

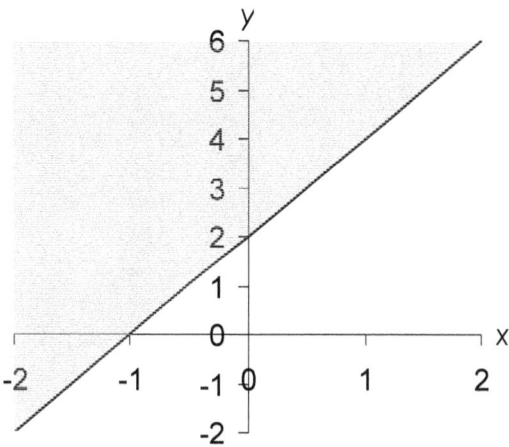

(Rigorous)

A. $y \leq -x + 2$

B. $y \geq 2x + 2$

C. $y = 2x + 2$

D. $y \geq 2x - 1$

Answer: B. $y \geq 2x + 2$

The shaded region includes all the points above the line. Thus, we need only find the equation for the line and then choose the correct symbol for the inequality. Note that the line has a slope of 2 (it increases by two units in the *y* direction for every one unit of increase in the *x* direction) and a *y*-intercept of 2. Thus, the equation for the line is

$y = 2x + 2$

Note that the shaded region is above the line; the best choice is then answer B, or $y \geq 2x + 2$.

18. Solve for L:

$$R = r + \frac{400(W-L)}{N}$$

(Rigorous) (Skill 6.6)

A. $\quad L = W - \dfrac{N}{400}(R-r)$

B. $\quad L = W + \dfrac{N}{400}(R-r)$

C. $\quad L = W - \dfrac{400}{N}(R-r)$

D. $\quad L = \dfrac{NR}{r} - 400W$

Answer: A. $L = W - \dfrac{N}{400}(R-r)$

$R = r + \dfrac{400(W-L)}{N}; \Rightarrow R - r = \dfrac{400(W-L)}{N}; \Rightarrow \dfrac{N}{400}(R-r) = W - L; \Rightarrow L = W - \dfrac{N}{400}(R-r)$

19. The formula for the volume of a cylinder is $V = \pi r^2 h$ where *r* is the radius of the cylinder and *h* is its height. What is the volume of a cylinder of diameter 2 cm and height 5 cm?
    (Average)

    A. $\quad 25\pi \, cm^2$

    B. $\quad 5\pi \, cm^2$

    C. $\quad 20\pi \, cm^2$

    D. $\quad 50\pi \, cm^2$

Answer: B. $5\pi \, cm^2$
Since the diameter of the cylinder is 2 cm, the radius is 1cm. Hence,

$V = \pi r^2 h = \pi(1)^2(5) = 5\pi \, cm^2$

20. The figure below is an equilateral triangle. Which transformation converts the solid-line figure to the broken-line figure?

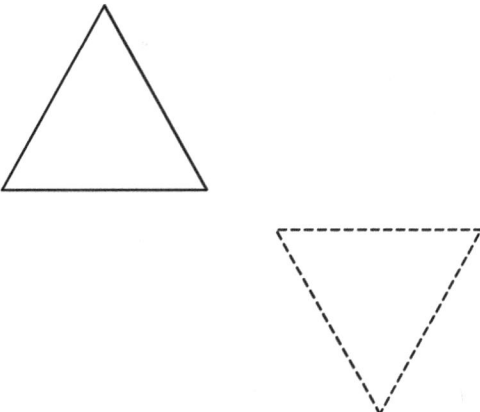

(Average)

A. Rotation

B. Reflection

C. Glide reflection

D. Any of the above

Answer: D. Any of the above

Because the triangle is equilateral, any of the geometric transformations listed above can be used to convert the solid-line triangle to the broken-line triangle. For a rotation, the center of rotation is chosen halfway between the two figures as shown below.

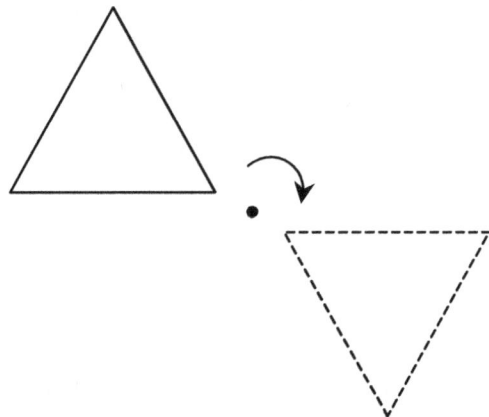

A reflection likewise requires a correctly chosen line of reflection, which acts like a mirror for the figure.

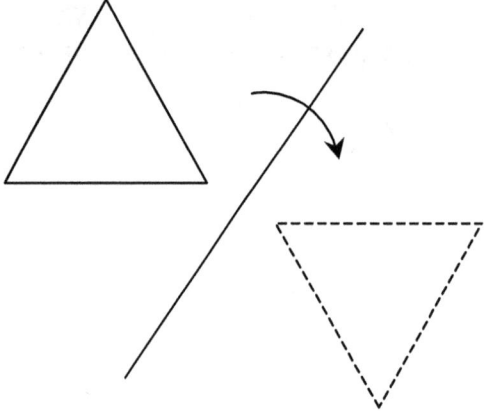

Finally, a glide reflection can also perform the transformation. A glide reflection is simply a translation followed by a reflection (or vice versa).

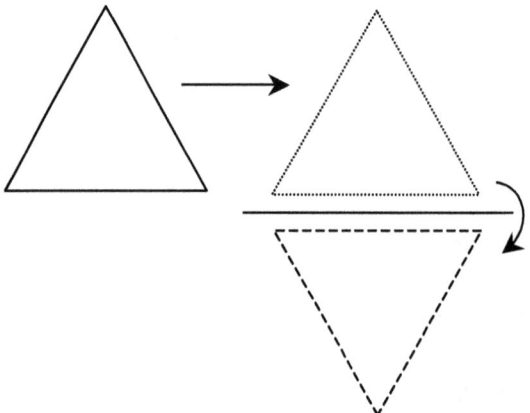

21. **Which of the following is a net of a cube?**
    (Rigorous)

    A.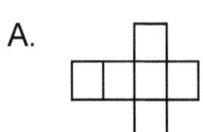

    B.

    C.

    D.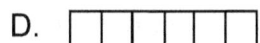

Answer: A.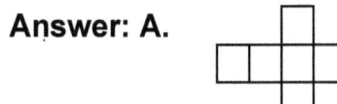

A net is a two-dimensional figure that can be folded (along the interior line segments) to form a three-dimensional figure of a specific type. Answer A is the only figure that is a net of a cube.

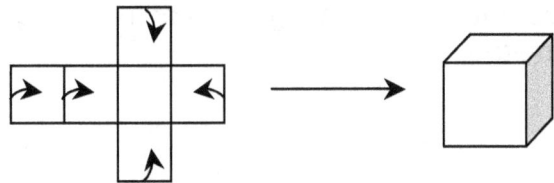

22. **What is the length of the shortest side of a right isosceles triangle if the longest side is 5 centimeters?**
    (Rigorous)

    A. 2.24 centimeters

    B. 2.5 centimeters

    C. 3.54 centimeters

    D. Not enough information

Answer: C. 3.54 centimeters
If a triangle is isosceles, then two of its sides are congruent, as are two of its angles. The longest side of such a triangle must be the hypotenuse; the other two sides, the legs, must be of equal length (this is because the congruent angles must be less than 90° each). Let's call the length of a leg x. Then, using the Pythagorean theorem,

$$x^2 + x^2 = 2x^2 = 5^2 = 25$$
$$x^2 = \frac{25}{2} = 12.5$$
$$x = \sqrt{12.5} \approx 3.54$$

Thus, the shortest side (the legs are congruent) of the triangle described in the problem is 3.54 centimeters.

23. What is the area of the shaded region below, where the circle has a radius *r*?

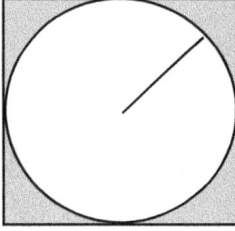

(Average)

A. r^2

B. $(4-\pi)r^2$

C. $(2-\pi)r^2$

D. $4\pi r^2$

Answer: B. $(4-\pi)r^2$

Notice that the figure is a circle of radius *r* inscribed in a quadrilateral—this quadrilateral must therefore be a square. Thus, the sides of the square each have a length twice that of the radius, as shown below.

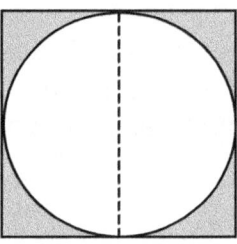 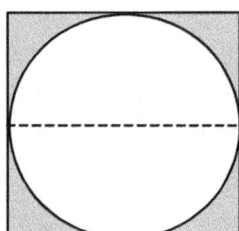

To find the area of the shaded region, subtract the area of the circle (πr^2) from the area of the square ($4r^2$).

$$A_{shaded} = 4r^2 - \pi r^2 = (4-\pi)r^2$$

24. The figure below is constructed with congruent equilateral triangles each having sides of length 4 units. What is the perimeter of the figure?

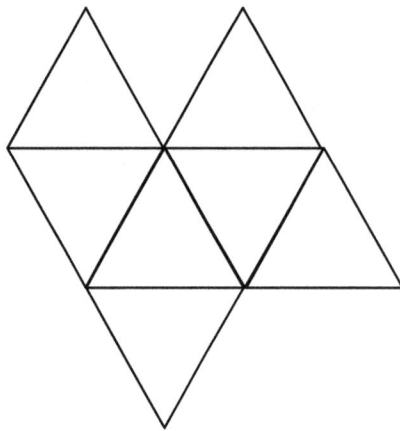

(Average)

A. 9 units

B. 36 units

C. 60 units

D. Not enough information

Answer: B. 36 units
To determine the perimeter, simply count the number of external sides of the figure and multiply the result by 4 units (each side of each triangle, according to the problem, has a length of 4 units). The figure has nine sides, so the perimeter is 36 units.

25. The following stem and leaf plot shows rainfall data in inches over several consecutive days. What is the median value?

0	7
1	3 9
2	1 5 7 8
3	0 3 4 6 6 9
4	3 5 5 7 8
5	0 0 3 5
10	3

(Average)

A. 3.6 in

B. 3.9 in

C. 4.3 in

D. 3.4 in

Answer: A. 3.9 in
Since there are 23 data points, the median or middle value is the 12th one.

26. A bag contains four red marbles and six blue marbles. If three selections are made without replacement, what is the probability of choosing three red marbles?
    (Rigorous)

    A.   3/10

    B.   8/125

    C.   1/30

    D.   1/60

Answer: C. 1/30
Because the question tells us that this experiment is performed without replacement, we know that each time a marble is chosen, it is not returned to the bag. In the first selection, the probability of choosing a red marble is 4 out of 10, or 2/5. In this case, a red marble is removed from the bag leaving three red marbles and six blue marbles. The probability of then making another selection of a red marble is three out of nine, or 1/3. This leaves two red marbles and six blue marbles. The probability of selecting a red marble in the final selection is then two out of eight, or 1/4. To determine the probability of these three selections occurring consecutively, we multiply the probabilities from each step.

$$P(\text{three red}) = \frac{2}{5} \cdot \frac{1}{3} \cdot \frac{1}{4} = \frac{2}{60} = \frac{1}{30}$$

Thus, we have a 1/30 chance of selecting (without replacement) three red marbles consecutively.

27. **What is the sample space for the sum of the outcomes for two rolls of a six-sided die?**
    (Average)

    A. {1, 2, 3, 4, 5, 6}

    B. {1, 2, 3, 4, 5, 6, 7, 8, 9, 10, 11, 12}

    C. {2, 3, 4, 5, 6, 7, 8, 9, 10, 11, 12}

    D. {7, 8, 9, 10, 11, 12}

Answer: C. {2, 3, 4, 5, 6, 7, 8, 9, 10, 11, 12}
A six-sided die can turn up any number between one and six, inclusive. The smallest sum that could be obtained from two rolls is for the case where both rolls turn up a one—the sum would then be two. The maximum sum would be the case where both rolls turn up a six—the sum would then be 12. Thus, the sample space for this experiment is 2 through 12, inclusive.

28. **How many different three-card hands can be drawn from a standard deck of 52 playing cards?**
    (Average)

    A. 156

    B. 2,704

    C. 132,600

    D. 140,608

Answer: C. 132,600
Each card in the deck is unique. To determine how many different three-card hands we could get, we need to multiply the number of possibilities for each card selection. In the first selection, we have 52 possible choices. In the second, we have 51 choices, and in the third, we have 50 choices. The number of possible hands, n, is the product of these three numbers.

$n = 52 \cdot 51 \cdot 50 = 132{,}600$

29. **How many ways can a card that is either red or a king be selected from a standard deck of 52 playing cards?**
    (Average)

    A.   26

    B.   28

    C.   30

    D.   104

Answer: B. 28
We want to know how many possible outcomes of a random selection from a deck are either red or a king. A 52-card deck contains 26 red cards and 4 kings; 2 of the kings, however, are red. In other words, these outcomes are not mutually exclusive. If we apply the addition principle of counting, then we find that the number of ways, n, that we can select a red card or king from the deck is

$n = 26 + 4 - 2 = 28$

The correct answer is thus B.

30. **A set of 5 positive integers has a mean of 7, median of 8 and mode of 9. What is the largest integer in the set?**
    (Rigorous)

    A.   12

    B.   8

    C.   9

    D.   10

Answer: C. 9
Since there are an odd number of integers, the median 8 must be the middle number. Since 9 is the mode, it must occur at least twice. Hence the last 3 integers in the set must be 8, 9, 9.

Answer Key: Math

1. D
2. B
3. D
4. C
5. A
6. C
7. D
8. A
9. D
10. A
11. D
12. B
13. B
14. A
15. C
16. B
17. B
18. A
19. B
20. D
21. A
22. C
23. B
24. B
25. A
26. C
27. C
28. C
29. B
30. C

Rigor Table: Math

	Easy 0%	Average 60%	Rigorous 40%
Questions		1, 2, 3, 4, 8, 9, 10, 11, 13, 15, 19, 20, 23, 24, 25, 27, 28, 29	5, 6, 7, 12, 14, 16, 17, 18, 21, 22, 26, 30

Math Essays

You have designed an alternative assessment based on a portfolio, observation, and oral presentation for a student with learning disabilities in the area of reading and writing. Your colleague is concerned that this lowers expectations for the student, deprives him of the chance to practice taking the kind of tests he needs to be successful, and sets him further apart from the other students.

Justify your choice of an alternative assessment for the learning-disabled student in place of the traditional tests that other students are taking. How would you respond to your colleague's concerns and reassure her that the assessment you are planning is valid and in the best interests of the student?

Sample Response

The primary purpose of assessment is to support the academic growth of a child. Thus assessment must provide an accurate picture of the skills and knowledge that a child has acquired. This goal overrides all other considerations, however valid they might be. The student who has difficulty with reading and writing will be at a disadvantage in a written and timed test. Thus, having him take the standard test with everyone will provide erroneous feedback about his real skills and understanding of content. The alternative assessment plan, on the other hand, gives the learning-disabled student an opportunity to show what he knows and gives the teacher more detailed and accurate feedback that can be used to modify and enhance the curriculum and teaching methods used for him. The portfolio and observation will allow the teacher to evaluate him based on multiple pieces of information gathered over a period of time. The oral presentation will allow him to express his knowledge using his strengths rather than his weaknesses. This will not only help him feel more confident and successful, it will help the teacher to better address his needs so that he can overcome his reading and writing difficulties in the long run.

My colleague's concerns are valid and must be kept in mind while planning a long-term approach to educating the learning-disabled student. While alternative assessments are called for in the short term, as the student progresses he must be trained and supported so that he is eventually able to take standard tests with other students. Care must be taken not to lower expectations in the alternative assessment. Clearly defined rubrics supporting high standards for the portfolio and oral presentation will ensure that this does not happen. The rubrics will be clearly explained to the student in advance. Finally, the goal of alternative assessment is to help the student's eventual integration with the rest of the class. It is his disability that currently sets him apart. A well-planned assessment structure feeding into enhanced instructional support will help close the gap.

SOCIAL SCIENCES

1. **Denver is called the "mile-high city" because it is:**
    (Average)

    A. Located approximately one mile above the plains of eastern Colorado

    B. Located exactly one mile above the base of Cheyenne Mountain

    C. Located approximately one mile above sea level

    D. The city with the tallest buildings in Colorado

Answer: C. Located approximately one mile above sea level
Elevations of cities are calculated according to the height above sea level. That fact negates all answers except C.

2. **The state of Louisiana is divided into parishes. What type of region do the parishes represent?**
    (Rigorous)

    A. Formal region

    B. Functional region

    C. Vernacular region

    D. Human region

Answer: A. Formal region
There are three main types of regions. Formal regions are areas defined by actual political boundaries, such as a city, county, or state. Functional regions are defined by a common function, such as the area covered by a telephone service. Vernacular regions are less formally defined areas that are formed by people's perception (e.g., "the Middle East" or "the South").

3. **Which continent is only one country?**
   (Average)

   A. Australia

   B. New Zealand

   C. The Arctic

   D. Antarctica

Answer: A. Australia
Of the seven continents, Australia is the only one that contains just one country. It is also the only island continent. Antarctica is the southernmost continent. It surrounds the South Pole. New Zealand is made up of two large islands, but it is not a continent. The Arctic is a region that includes parts of several continents, but is not in and of itself a continent. In fact, much of the Arctic is ice-covered ocean.

4. **The Southern Hemisphere contains all of which continent?**
   (Rigorous)

   A. Africa

   B. Australia

   C. South America

   D. North America

Answer: B. Australia
The Southern Hemisphere, located between the South Pole and the Equator, contains all of Australia, a small part of Asia, about one-third of Africa, most of South America, and all of Antarctica.

5. Anthropology is:
   (Average)

   A. The profession that made the Leakey family famous

   B. The scientific study of human culture and humanity

   C. Not related to geography at all

   D. Margaret Mead's study of the Samoans

Answer: B. The scientific study of human culture and humanity
Anthropology did make the Leakeys famous (choice A) but that does not define anthropology. The text states that anthropology is related to geography (choice C). Margaret Mead's study of the Samoans (choice D) is only one part of anthropology.

6. In the 1920s, Margaret Mead wrote *Coming of Age in Samoa*, relating her observations about this group's way of life. What of these types of geographical study best describes her method?
   (Rigorous)

   A. Regional

   B. Topical

   C. Physical

   D. Human

Answer: D. Human
Mead studied the Samoans' human activity patterns and how they related to the environment including political, cultural, historical, urban, and social geographical fields of study. Regional study is limited to the elements and characteristics of a place or region. In a topical, a research would focus on an earth feature or one human activity occurring throughout the entire world. In a physical study, the researcher would focus on the earth's physical features and what creates and changes them, how they relate to each other and to human activities.

7. Which activity is most likely to have a negative environmental impact on an area?
(Rigorous)

   I. Building a new skyscraper in Manhattan
   II. Strip mining for coal in West Virginia
   III. Digging a new oil well within an existing oilfield in Texas
   IV. Building ten new homes in a 100-acre suburban neighborhood that already contains fifty homes

   A. II and III only

   B. II only

   C. I only

   D. I and IV only

Answer: B. II only
Strip mining sometimes involves using dynamite to remove the top of a mountain and is thus very harmful to an environment. In regard to oil wells and skyscrapers; building one new oil well in an existing oilfield or one new skyscraper in Manhattan (which already has a high concentration of skyscrapers) won't make an extremely heavy environmental impact. Building the ten new homes in an existing neighborhood where there is plenty of room for expansion will probably have only a modest environmental impact.

8. Which of the following are two agricultural innovations that began in China?
(Average)

   A. Using pesticides and fertilizer

   B. Irrigation and cuneiform

   C. Improving the silk industry and inventing gunpowder

   D. Terrace farming and crop rotation

Answer: D. Terrace farming and crop rotation
Pesticides and fertilizer (choice A) are modern innovations. It was the Sumerians who introduced irrigation and cuneiform (choice B), not the Chinese. The Chinese did improve the silk industry and invent gunpowder (choice C), but these are not agricultural innovations.

9. **Which civilization laid the foundations of geometry?**
   (Average)

   A. Egyptian

   B. Greek

   C. Roman

   D. Chinese

Answer: B. Greek
In the field of mathematics, Pythagoras and Euclid laid the foundation of geometry and Archimedes calculated the value of *pi* during the Ancient Greek civilization. Egypt made numerous significant contributions, including the invention of the method of counting in groups of 1–10 (the decimal system). The contributions and accomplishments of the Romans are numerous, but their greatest included language, engineering, building, law, government, roads, trade, and the "Pax Romana," the long period of peace enabling free travel and trade, spreading people, cultures, goods, and ideas all over a vast area of the known world. The Chinese studied nature and weather; stressed the importance of education, family, and a strong central government; followed the religions of Buddhism, Confucianism, and Taoism; and invented such things as gunpowder, paper, printing, and the magnetic compass.

10. **The international organization established to work for world peace at the end of the Second World War is the:**
    (Average)

    A. League of Nations

    B. United Federation of Nations

    C. United Nations

    D. United World League

Answer: C United Nations
The international organization established to work for world peace at the end of the Second World War was the United Nations. From the ashes of the failed League of Nations, established following World War I, the United Nations continues to be a major player in world affairs today.

11. In December, Ms. Griffin asks her students to talk about their holiday traditions. Rebecca explains about lighting the nine candles during Chanukkah, Josh explains about the lighting of the seven candles during Kwanzaa, and Bernard explains about lighting the four candles during Advent. This is an example of:
    (Rigorous)

    A. Cross-cultural exchanges

    B. Cultural diffusion

    C. Cultural identity

    D. Cosmopolitanism

Answer: C. Cross-cultural exchanges
Cross-cultural exchanges involved the discovery of shared values and needs as well as an appreciation of differences. Cultural diffusion is the movement of cultural ideas or materials between populations independent of the movement of those populations. Cultural identity is the identification of individuals or groups as they are influenced by their belonging to a particular group or culture. Cosmopolitanism blurs cultural differences in the creation of a shared new culture.

12. English and Spanish colonists took what from Native Americans?
    (Average)

    A. Land

    B. Water rights

    C. Money

    D. Religious beliefs

Answer: A. Land
The settlers took a lot of land from the Native Americans. Water rights (choice B), money (choice C), and religious beliefs (choice D) are not mentioned as areas of contention between the European settlers and the Native Americans.

13. **Spanish colonies were:**
    (Average)

    A.   Mainly in the northeast

    B.   Mainly in the south

    C.   Mainly in the Midwest

    D.   Mainly in Canada

Answer: B. Mainly in the south
English colonies were in the northeast (choice A). What is now the Midwest (choice C) had not yet been settled by Europeans. French colonies were in "the extreme north," which is present-day Canada (choice D).

14. **In the events leading up to the American Revolution, which of these methods was effective in dealing with the British taxes?**
    (Rigorous)

    A.   Boycotts

    B.   Strikes

    C.   Armed conflicts

    D.   Resolutions

Answer: A. Boycotts
In several instances, boycotts were effective in convincing the British to repeat taxes. For example in 1765, merchants boycotted imported English goods, and the Stamp Act was repealed three months later. In 1767, boycotts led to the repeal of the Townshend Acts. Strikes were not a factor. Armed conflicts tended to strengthen British resolve and resolutions had no weight. Boycotts affected the British economy and achieved greater success for the colonies.

15. One of the political parties that developed in the early 1790s was led by:
(Rigorous)

- A. Thomas Jefferson
- B. George Washington
- C. Aaron Burr
- D. John Quincy Adams

Answer: A. Thomas Jefferson.
George Washington (choice B) "warned against the creation of 'factions.'" Aaron Burr (choice C) is the man who killed Alexander Hamilton in a duel. John Quincy Adams (choice D) was not active in politics until the 1820s.

16. How did the labor force change after 1830?
(Average)

- A. Employers began using children
- B. Employers began hiring immigrants
- C. Employers began hiring women
- D. Employers began hiring non-immigrant men

Answer: B. Employers began hiring immigrants
Employers began hiring immigrants who were arriving in large numbers. Children (choice A) and women (choice C) began entering the labor force prior to 1830. Employers had always used non-immigrant men (choice D).

17. Which of these was not a result of World War I in the United States?
    (Average)

    A. Establishment of new labor laws.

    B. Prosperous industrial growth.

    C. Formation of the United Nations

    D. Growth of the stock market.

Answer: C. Formation of the United Nations
The United Nations was formed after World War II. After World War I, the League of Nations formed and established the United States in a central position in international relations that would increase in importance through the century.

18. Among civilized people:
    (Average)

    A. Strong government is not necessary

    B. Systems of control are rudimentary at best

    C. Government has no sympathy for individuals or for individual happiness

    D. Governments began to assume more institutional forms

Answer: D. Governments began to assume more institutional forms
Absence of strong government (choice A) is harmful. Systems of government that are rudimentary at best (choice B) are not suitable for civilized people. It is not true that government among civilized people has no sympathy for individuals or for individual happiness (choice C).

19. **The U.S. House of Representatives has:**
    (Average)

    A. 100 members

    B. 435 members

    C. Three branches

    D. A president and a vice president

Answer: B. 435 members
The U.S. Senate has 100 members (choice A). The U.S. government as a whole has three branches (choice C). The executive branch of the U.S. government has a president and a vice-president (choice D).

20. **Socialism is:**
    (Rigorous)

    A. A system of government with a legislature

    B. A system where the government is subject to a vote of "no confidence"

    C. A political belief and system in which the state takes a guiding role in the national economy

    D. A system of government with three distinct branches

Answer: C. A political belief and system in which the state takes a guiding role in the national economy
Socialism does not involve a legislature (choice A). A vote of "no confidence" (choice B) is associated with a parliamentary system, not with socialism. The U.S. government has three branches (choice D). This is not socialism.

21. **Which of the following was not a source of conflict in writing the U.S. Constitution?**
    (Average)

    A. Establishing a monarchy

    B. Equalizing power between the small states and the large states

    C. Dealing with slavery

    D. Electing a president

Answer: A. Establishing a monarchy.
Although the British system of government was the basis of the U.S. Constitution, the delegates to the Constitutional Convention were divided on the way power would be held. Some wanted a strong, centralized, individual authority. Others feared autocracy or the growth of monarchy. The compromise was to give the president broad powers but to limit the amount of time, through term of office, that any individual could exercise that power.

22. **In 2002, then-President George W. Bush briefly transferred his presidential power to Vice President Dick Cheney for about an hour while undergoing a colonoscopy. Under what amendment was this covered?**
    (Rigorous)

    A. The Nineteenth Amendment

    B. The Twentieth Amendment

    C. The Twenty-second Amendment

    D. The Twenty-fifth Amendment

Answer: D. The Twenty-fifth Amendment
Presidential succession is the focus of the Twenty-fifth Amendment, which provides a blueprint of what to do if the president is incapacitated or killed. The long battle for voting rights for women ended in success with the passage of the Nineteenth Amendment. The date for the beginning of terms for the President and the Congress was changed from March to January by the Twentieth Amendment. The Twenty-second Amendment limited the number of terms that a President could serve to two.

23. **Upon arrest, a person is read a "Miranda warning" which reads, in part, "You have the right to remain silent. Anything you say can and will be used against you in a court of law." Under what amendment in the Bill of Rights is this covered?**
    (Rigorous)

    A. The right against unreasonable search and seizures

    B. The right to trial by jury and right to legal council

    C. The right against self-incrimination

    D. The right to jury trial for civil actions

Answer: C. The right against self-incrimination
According to the Fifth Amendment, a citizen has the privilege to prevent self-incrimination. Law enforcement officials advise a suspect in custody of his/her right to remain silent. While the right to council is also part of the Miranda warning, it is not part of the question as written here.

24. **The equilibrium price:**
    (Rigorous)

    A. Is the price that clears the markets

    B. Is the price in the middle

    C. Identifies a shortage or a surplus

    D. Is an agricultural price support

Answer: A. Is the price that clears the markets.
The price in the middle (choice B) is related to the principle of equilibrium, but it is not the equilibrium price. The equilibrium price has no direct connection to shortages and surpluses (choice C). It is also not an agricultural price support (choice D).

25. **Capital is:**
    (Rigorous)

    A. Anyone who sells his or her ability to produce goods and services

    B. The ability of an individual to combine the three inputs with his or her own talents to produce a viable good or service

    C. Anything that is manufactured to be used in the production process

    D. The land itself and everything occurring naturally on it

Answer: C. Anything that is manufactured to be used in the production process

Anyone who sells his or her ability to produce goods and services (choice A) is labor, not capital. Combining three inputs with one's own talents to produce a viable good or service (choice B) is related to entrepreneurship. The land (choice D) and what is on it pertains to land.

26. **Which of the following countries has historically operated in a market economy?**
    (Rigorous)

    A. Great Britain

    B. Cuba

    C. Yugoslavia

    D. India

Answer: A. Great Britain

A market economy is based on supply and demand and the use of markets. While Great Britain may have socialized medicine, it operates a market economy. Cuba, with its ties to Communism, has a centrally planned economy. Historically, China has had a centrally planned economy but is now moving towards a market economy. Yugoslavia was a market socialist economy, but the country no longer exists; it has been split into Montenegro and Serbia.

27. For their research paper on the use of technology in the classroom, students have gathered data that shows a sharp increase in the number of online summer classes over the past five years. What would be the best way for them to depict this information visually?
    (Average)

    A.   A line chart

    B.   A table

    C.   A pie chart

    D.   A flow chart

Answer: A. A line chart
A line chart is used to show trends over time and will emphasize the sharp increase. A table is appropriate to show the exact numbers but does not have the same impact as a line chart. Not appropriate are a pie chart that shows the parts of a whole or a flow chart that details processes or procedures.

28. An example of something that is not a primary source is:
    (Average)

    A.   The published correspondence between Winston Churchill and Franklin D. Roosevelt during World War II

    B.   Martin Gilbert's biography of Winston Churchill

    C.   The diary of Field Marshal Sir Alan Brooke, the head of the British Army
          during World War II

    D.   Franklin D. Roosevelt's handwritten notes from the World War II era

Answer: B. Martin Gilbert's biography of Winston Churchill
Martin Gilbert's biography of Winston Churchill is a secondary source because it was not written by Churchill himself. The Churchill-Roosevelt correspondence, Brooke's diary, and FDR's handwritten notes are all primary source documents written by actual historical figures.

29. Mr. Phillips is creating a unit to study *To Kill a Mockingbird* and wants to familiarize his high school freshmen with the attitudes and issues of the historical period. Which activity would familiarize students with the attitudes and issues of the Depression-era South?
(Rigorous)

	A.	Create a detailed timeline of 15–20 social, cultural, and political events that focus on race relations in the 1930s

	B.	Research and report on the life of its author Harper Lee; compare her background with the events in the book

	C.	Watch the movie version and note language and dress

	D.	Write a research report on the stock market crash of 1929 and its effects

Answer: A. Create a detailed timeline of 15–20 social, cultural, and political events that focus on race relations in the 1930s
By identifying the social, cultural, and political events of the 1930s, students will better understand the attitudes and values of America during the time of the novel. While researching the author's life could add depth to their understanding of the novel, it is unnecessary to the appreciation of the novel by itself. The movie version is an accurate depiction of the novel's setting, but it focuses on the events in the novel, not the external factors that fostered the conflict. The stock market crash and the subsequent Great Depression would be important to note on the timeline but students would be distracted from themes of the book by narrowing their focus to only these two events.

30. Which of the following is not an excellent way to teach students about World War II?
(Rigorous)

    A.   To ask a World War II veteran to visit your class and talk to students about the war

    B.   To have students read books on World War II

    C.   To have students read primary source materials on World War II, such as the text of the Atlantic Charter

    D.   To have students watch the movie *Schindler's List*

Answer: D To have students watch the movie *Schindler's List*.
To have students watch the movie *Schindler's List*, a movie that portrays one small aspect of the Holocaust in which hope for the future was a possibility for a small group of Jews. In actuality, and as a whole, the Holocaust was about the mass murder of millions of people who had no opportunity to hope for a better future. Listening to a World War II veteran speak or reading books and/or primary sources about the war are excellent ways to learn about World War II.

Answer Key: Social Sciences

1. C
2. A
3. A
4. B
5. B
6. D
7. B
8. D
9. B
10. C
11. C
12. C
13. A
14. B
15. A

16. B
17. C
18. D
19. B
20. C
21. A
22. D
23. C
24. A
25. C
26. A
27. A
28. B
29. A
30. D

Rigor Table: Social Sciences

	Easy 0%	Average 50%	Rigorous 50%
Questions	0	1, 3, 5, 8, 9, 10, 12, 13, 16, 17, 18, 19, 21, 27, 28	2, 4, 6, 7, 11, 14, 15, 20, 22, 23, 24, 25, 26, 29, 30

Social Sciences Essays

You are an elementary school teacher at a Title 1 school. Your school district has been unable to purchase new textbooks for your school in several years. Because of that, the Social Studies textbooks in your classroom are becoming quickly out-dated, and there are no supplemental materials to use for hands-on learning. Along with teaching the content Social Studies standards, you also have to be sure that your students are learning Historical and Social Science Analysis Skills that are often overlooked because of a lack of resources. These skills are not only an important aspect of creating independent thinkers in your classroom, they are also important to making Social Studies come alive for the students, to becoming relevant in their own lives. Being that you only have older Social Studies textbooks at your disposal and no additional resources in the classroom, you have to think "out of the box" to teach these analysis skills to your students.

Historical and Social Science Analysis Skills for grades K–5 include such ideas as:
- Chronological and Spatial Thinking
    - interpreting time lines
    - using terms related to time
    - connections between past and present
    - interpretation of maps and globes, and significance of location
- Research, Evidence, and Point of View
    - differentiation between primary and secondary sources
    - posing relevant questions about events and sources
    - distinguishing between fact and fiction
- Historical Interpretation
    - summarize key events and explain historical context of those events
    - identify human and physical characteristics of places and explain how these are unique to such places
    - identify and interpret multiple causes and effects of events

Given the above information and circumstance, create instructional strategies/activities to teach 2 to 3 of the Historical and Social Science Analysis Skills outlined above. These skills can be taught using any Social Studies content and are for grades K–5 as noted above.

Sample Response

The Historical and Social Science Analysis Skills can seem to be quite daunting to a classroom teacher, especially one with limited resources available. I understand, though, the importance of these skills in creating independent thinkers. I can also see how easily these skills can be brushed aside, leaving teachers to rely on and solely teach from a Social Studies textbook. I believe that Social Studies will only become relevant to students if these analysis skills are included in the teaching of the curriculum; they truly make the content come alive for the students. Considering that these skills are concurrent for grades K–5, it is important to start with simple, uncomplicated activities for the lower grades and then build to more complex activities for the upper grades. This idea is the basis of the activities described below.

For the analysis skill of distinguishing between fact and fiction:
- In Kindergarten, students learn about important historical legends and figures, such as Pocahontas and Benjamin Franklin. I will begin with reading to the students from the textbook. Then, as a class, we will discuss and make a list of why these figures are important. I will then read a fictional story about the figure to the class. We will then talk about the differences between the reading from the text and the fictional story. This will begin a continuing discussion between things that are fact and things that are fiction.
- In 2nd grade, students again learn about important historical figures and how they've made differences for us today. Similar activities can be used to review this analysis skill at the start of the school year. To further the students' understanding of this skill, another activity will involve a more hands on approach. The class will be divided into teams of 4. Each team will be assigned a historical figure from the textbook. They will then have to locate a storybook on that person in the library. The team will read aloud to the class information from the text and information from the storybook. On a T-chart, their classmates will write down what they believe to be factual information and fictional information. These T-charts will be shared with the class and the presenting team will lead a discussion regarding which information was factual and which was fictional.

For the analysis skill of making connections between the past and the present:
- In 1st grade, students study transportation methods of the past. To introduce this information, I will show students pictures of various modes of transportation throughout history. I will present these pictures in chronological order and lead a discussion of what life must have been like with these transportation methods. This will continue throughout the week as we reach more current methods of transportation. At the conclusion of this lesson, students will choose one of the modes of transportation and in

a paragraph, write about how they think their life would have been like if that was the way their family got around. Then, the students will share their paragraphs with the class. We will then discuss how different life would be if we still used that type of transportation. This series of lessons will conclude with a discussion of why changes have been made in transportation as time progressed.
- In 2nd grade, students compare/contrast their own lives with their parents and grandparents. To continue the study of making connections between the past and the present, students will begin the school year by creating a storyboard of their own life, including such things as clothes that are worn, modes of transportation, life at home, and life at school. This activity will be followed by creating a storyboard of the life of a grandparent or other elderly relative with the same categories. Students will then compare/contrast their storyboards. Choosing to either live as a child when their grandparent or relative did or to have their grandparent or relative be a child now, the students will write a story about what that life would be like, how it would be different. This series of activities will conclude with a class discussion about why some things have changed and some have not. These types of lessons could continue in 3rd grade when the students learn about the development of their communities.

One of the many great things about teaching the Historical and Social Sciences Analysis Skills is that they can so easily build upon each other and add depth to the content of textbooks. I believe that once a teacher begins to teach these skills in their classrooms, the skills become more easily integrated into everyday Social Studies lessons.

SCIENCE

1. Which of the following layers comprises the earth's plates?
   (Easy)

   A. Mesosphere

   B. Troposphere

   C. Asthensophere

   D. Lithosphere

Answer: D. Lithosphere
The lithosphere is made up of the crust and the upper mantle. The lithosphere "floats" on the asthensophere, causing the plates to move across the earth's surface.

2. The Himalayas, a folded mountain range, have formed at a:
   (Average)

   A. Divergent plate boundary

   B. A continental- oceanic convergent plate boundary

   C. An oceanic -oceanic convergent plate boundary

   D. A continental-continental convergent plate boundary

Answer: D. A continental-continental convergent plate boundary
Two continental plates push together to form folded mountains. Continental plates do not subduct. Therefore, volcanic mountains are not found at continental convergent plate boundaries.

3. **What conditions are required to create coarse-grained igneous rocks?**
   (Average)

   A. High temperature and pressure

   B. Slowly cooling magma

   C. Quickly cooling lava

   D. Evaporation and cementation

Answer: B. Slowly cooling magma
Igneous rocks are formed from cooling magma and lava. Lava that cools quickly forms fine-grained or glassy igneous rocks, as crystals do not have a chance to form. Magma that cools slowly forms coarse-grained igneous rocks as the crystals are given time to form.

4. **Which of the following describes the law of superposition?**
   (Easy)

   A. The present is the key to the past

   B. The oldest rocks in a rock unit are found on the top of the rock column

   C. The oldest rocks in a rock unit are found on the bottom of the rock column

   D. Faults that cut across rock units are younger than the units they cut across

Answer: C. The oldest rocks in a rock unit are found on the bottom of the rock column
Sediments are deposited and cemented on top of old deposits. Therefore the oldest rocks are at the bottom of a column, and the youngest rocks are at the top of a column.

5. **How are igneous, metamorphic, and sedimentary rocks classified?**
   (Average)

   A.   The chemical composition of the rocks

   B.   When the rocks were formed

   C.   How the rocks were formed

   D.   The location of the rocks within the Earth's crust

The correct answer is C. How the rocks were formed
Igneous rocks are the result of cooling molten rock, or magma. Sedimentary rocks are created when small rock particles are cemented together. Metamorphic rocks are igneous rocks, sedimentary rocks, or metamorphic rocks that are transformed by heat and pressure.

6. **In which period did land animals first appear?**
   (Easy)

   A.   350 to 135 million years ago

   B.   Devonian

   C.   Paleozoic

   D.   Cretaceous

Answer: B. Devonian
Periods and eras are defined by certain events. The Paleozoic era includes five periods, one of which is the Devonian period. In the Devonian period, insects and amphibians appeared. The Cretaceous period is from 135 million years ago to 65 million years ago.

7. **Which era had dinosaurs in it?**
   (Easy)

   A. Cenozoic

   B. Mesozoic

   C. Triassic

   D. Paleozoic

Answer: B. Mesozoic
The Cenozoic era began with the appearance of mammals and birds. Insects appeared on land in the Paleozoic era. The Mesozoic era includes the Cretaceous, Jurassic, and Triassic periods.

8. **Which of the following objects in the universe is the largest?**
   (Average)

   A. Pulsars

   B. Quasars

   C. Black holes

   D. Nebulas

Answer: B. Quasars
Pulsars are neutron stars. Black holes are stars that have become so dense that light can't escape from the surface. Quasars appear to be stars but are distant galaxies. Nebulas are clouds of dust and gas that give rise to stars under the force of gravity.

9. **Why is the northern winter slightly warmer than the southern winter?**
   (Average)

   A. Because the perihelion occurs in January

   B. Because of global warming

   C. Because there is more water in the southern hemisphere

   D. Because Earth rotates on an axis that is not perpendicular to the plane of rotation

Answer: A. Because the perihelion occurs in January
Choice D explains why there are seasons; that is, why in the northern hemisphere January is colder than July and in the southern hemisphere July is colder than January. However, Earth travels in an elliptical path. It is closer to the sun in January than in July.

10. **What are ribosomes?**
    (Easy)

    A. Contain digestive enzymes that break down food

    B. Where proteins are synthesized

    C. Make ATP

    D. Hold stored food

Answer: B. Where proteins are synthesized
Vacuoles store food and pigments and are large in plants. Mitochondria are the organelles that produce ATP for energy. Lysosomes contain digestive enzymes and are found mainly in animals.

11. The role of rough endoplasmic reticulum is:
    (Easy)

    A. Metabolic functions

    B. Produce lipids

    C. Produce enzymes

    D. Protein synthesis

Answer: D. Protein synthesis
Rough endoplasmic reticulum (ER) synthesizes proteins such as hormones secreted outside the body. Smooth ER produces lipids. Mitochondria help with metabolic functions and the lysosomes produce enzymes.

12. What is the purpose of sexual reproduction?
    (Rigorous)

    A. Produce more organisms

    B. Produce organisms that are genetically diverse

    C. Give organisms the protection of male and female parents

    D. Increase social cooperation between organisms

Answer: B. Produce organisms that are genetically diverse
Single-celled organisms reproduce by cell division and somatic cells in a multicellular organism reproduce the same way (mitosis). The purpose of sex is to produce diverse offspring so that the offspring have a better chance of surviving. In meiosis, the chromosome number is half the number in the parent cell, so that there is genetic diversity when the sex cells recombine.

13. **In mitotic cell division, at what stage do the chromosomes line up in the cell?**
    (Average)

    A. Interphase

    B. Anaphase

    C. Prophase

    D. Metaphase

Answer: D. Metaphase
The interphase is the period before mitosis begins. In the anaphase, the chromosomes are pulled apart. In the prophase, the chromatin condenses to become visible chromosomes.

14. **Oogenesis is the formation of:**
    (Easy)

    A. Eggs

    B. Sperm

    C. Pollen

    D. Cytoplasm

Answer: A. Eggs
Oogenesis is the formation of eggs. Spermatogenesis is the formation of sperm.

15. **According to natural selection:**
    (Easy)

    A. Individuals within a population are identical

    B. Those with better traits have less offspring

    C. Successive generations will possess better traits

    D. Single individuals evolve to fit their surroundings

Answer: C. Successive generations will possess better traits
Organisms that possess better traits in order for survival tend to have greater numbers of offspring. These traits get passed down from generation to generation, causing later generations to possess the better traits.

16. **Chemicals released by an organism as way of communicating are called:**
    (Easy)

    A. Pheromones

    B. Synapses

    C. Chemoreceptors

    D. Thermoreceptors

Answer: A. Synapses
Pheromones are released by organisms for communication purposes. Animals may use them to attract a mate or use them as a warning signal.

17. **Which of the following is not a kingdom in the classification of living organisms?**
    (Average)

    A.   Plants

    B.   Fungi

    C.   Viruses

    D.   Bacteria

Answer: C. Viruses
Viruses do not obtain nutrients from their environment and produce new materials. The other kingdoms are animals and protists. Protists are single-celled organisms with nuclei, and bacteria do not have nuclei.

18. **Which property do plants have that fungi do not have?**
    (Average)

    A.   Sexual reproduction

    B.   Photosynthesis

    C.   Digestion

    D.   Locomotion

Answer: B. Photosynthesis
Fungi get their nutrients from other organisms by digestion. Locomotion is a characteristic of animals.

19. Which term describes the relationship between barnacles and whales?
    (Rigorous)

    A. Commensalism

    B. Parasitism

    C. Competition

    D. Mutualism

Answer: A. Commensalism
Barnacles need to attach themselves to a hard surface to survive. They benefit from being attached to whales. If the whales benefited too, the relationship would be mutualism. If the whales were harmed, the barnacles would be parasites. If they ate the same food, there would be competition.

20. Which of the following describes the transformation of liquid water to ice?
    (Average)

    A. Chemical change

    B. Physical change

    C. Thermodynamic change

    D. Non-chemical molecular change

Answer: B. Physical change
Since heat is taken away, it could be called a thermodynamic change. However, a change in state or phase is considered a physical change. It is more closely related to changing wood into saw dust then burning wood.

21. **Will Lithium gain or lose an electron when forming an ion? How many electrons will it gain or lose?**
    (Average)

    A.   Gain 1

    B.   Gain 2

    C.   Lose 1

    D.   Lose 2

Answer: C. Lose 1
Lithium will lose 1 electron to form an ion. Lithium has a lone electron in its outer shell. Atoms want to be stable by having their outer shells full. It is easier for lithium to lose 1 electron, thereby knocking off an entire shell, then to gain 7 more electrons to fill its outer shell.

22. **On which of the following does the force of friction between a metal stool and a wooden floor not depend?**
    (Rigorous)

    A.   The speed of the chair

    B.   Whether the stool has three legs or four

    C.   The type of metal

    D.   The smoothness of the floor

Answer: B. Whether the stool has three legs or four
The frictional force depends only on the force between the two surfaces and the nature of the two surfaces. Choice A is wrong because static friction is greater than moving friction. The number of legs determines the area of contact.

23. Which of the following laws implies that the force on an object comes from another object?
    (Average)

    A. Newton's first law of motion

    B. Newton's second law of motion

    C. Newton's third law of motion

    D. Coulomb's law

Answer: C. Newton's third law of motion
Newton's second law states the connection between force and acceleration. Newton's first law says if there is no force there will be no acceleration. Coulomb's law and the law of gravity says what the force between two objects will be. Newton's third law says forces come in pairs, which implies that the force comes from another object.

24. Which of the following quantities has the units of calories per degree?
    (Easy)

    A. Heat capacity

    B. Specific heat

    C. Heat equivalent

    D. Heat transfer

Answer: A. Heat capacity
Heat capacity is how much the temperature of an object will increase when a quantity of heat is added to the object. The specific heat is the heat capacity divided by the mass.

25. **How does a steam radiator deliver heat energy to a room?**
    (Rigorous)

    A. Radiation

    B. Conduction

    C. Convection

    D. Contact

Answer: C. Convection
While the radiator gets hot from the steam the amount of infrared radiation it emits into the room is small. Contact is the same as conduction. There is very little conduction of heat because air is a good insulator. Air very close to the radiator will get hot, but nearby air will not. The air near the radiator expands and rises. New cooler air replaces the hot rising air. As a result, the room reaches a higher temperature.

26. **What kind of chemical reaction is photosynthesis?**
    (Rigorous)

    A. Fusion

    B. Exothermic

    C. Endothermic

    D. Could be exothermic or endothermic

Answer: D. Could be exothermic or endothermic
Photosynthesis combines oxygen with carbon. When carbon burns heat is given off, so combining carbon and oxygen is exothermic. But with photosynthesis, radiant energy is used. Fusion refers to the combining of nuclei, not atoms.

27. A controlled experiment with tomato plants was conducted to see if the amount of water given to the plants affected the number of tomatoes grown. One plant was given 1 gallon of water, another 2 gallons, another 3 gallons, etc. The number of tomatoes produced for each plant was measured. What was the controlled variable?
(Average)

   A.   Type of plant

   B.   Amount of water

   C.   Number of tomatoes

   D.   Amount of fertilizer

Answer: A. Type of plant
The amount of water is the independent variable, and the number of tomatoes is the dependent variable. Each time the same type of plant was used, which meant there were only two variables in the experiment. Presumably, the amount of fertilizer was also controlled, but the question did not mention fertilizer.

28. Which of the following should be limited in a balanced diet?
(Easy)

   A.   Carbohydrates

   B.   Fats and oils

   C.   Proteins

   D.   Vitamins

Answer: B. Fats and oils
Fats and oils should be used in moderation. Saturated fats can lead to heart disease and high cholesterol.

29. **Which of the following statements about scientific knowledge best explains what scientific knowledge is?**
    (Average)

    A.   Scientific knowledge is based on experiments

    B.   Science knowledge is empirical

    C.   Scientific knowledge is tentative

    D.   Scientific knowledge is based on reason

Answer: B. Science knowledge is empirical
Experiments involve observing two quantities to determine the relationship between them. Observing means gaining knowledge from one of the five senses, which is another word for *empirical knowledge.* Scientific knowledge in some areas is tentative because new and different observations are always possible. Science is based on reason, but so are other types of knowledge.

30. **An experiment is performed to determine the effects of acid rain on plant life. Which of the following would be the variable?**
    (Average)

    A.   The type of plant

    B.   The amount of light

    C.   The pH of the water

    D.   The amount of water

Answer: C. The pH of the water
The variable is the value that is manipulated during the experiment. In order to determine proper cause and effect, the plant type, light, and amount of water should be kept the same for various plants, and the pH of the water should change.

Answer Key: Science

1. D	16. A
2. D	17. C
3. B	18. B
4. C	19. A
5. C	20. B
6. B	21. C
7. B	22. B
8. B	23. C
9. A	24. A
10. B	25. C
11. D	26. D
12. B	27. A
13. D	28. B
14. A	29. B
15. C	30. C

Rigor Table: Science

	Easy 36.7%	Average 46.7%	Rigorous 16.6%
Questions	1, 4, 6, 7, 10, 11, 14, 15, 16, 24, 28	2, 3, 5, 8, 9, 13, 17, 18, 20, 21, 23, 27, 29, 30	12, 19, 22, 25, 26

Science Essays

A mechanical wave is a disturbance in a medium in which energy is propagated but not bulk matter. Waves can be transverse or longitudinal. A wave has frequency, amplitude, and wavelength. The speed of a wave is determined by the medium.

What would be the instructional objective, lesson motivation, and student activity in a lesson about waves?

Sample Response

The instructional objective is that students will learn that waves travel in a medium and have a speed, amplitude, and frequency. A motivation should give students an incentive or reason to be interested in the lesson. The lesson can be motivated by asking students what sound is. Also, you can demonstrate a mechanical wave by sending a series of pulses down a Slinky or a long spring. Send a single longitudinal pulse down a Slinky by compressing it over a small distance and releasing the deformation. Ask students what is moving and why. Demonstrate a transverse pulse and ask students to describe the difference. Use a different medium, such as a rope, to show different media have different speeds. The speed of a wave traveling down a spring can be increased by giving the spring different tensions. Elicit from students why the speed of the wave changes. Set up standing waves in a spring by sending waves in opposite directions. Discuss with students whether or not a standing wave is a wave or a vibration.

www.ingramcontent.com/pod-product-compliance
Lightning Source LLC
LaVergne TN
LVHW061313060426
835507LV00019B/2133